Under the pen name of 'Stonie', John Stoneham has been published in the motoring and motorsport media for some 40 years. In parallel to cartoon, caricature and illustration work, active participation in motor sport event organisation has provided a backdrop to a career that started at a local speedway in his home city of Adelaide, South Australia. Dabbling in motor sport competition as a privateer in many classic car events over the years, then as a media participant, the cartoonist moved into major work with key sponsors and factory race teams. After a brief period working in London in the late seventies, the young illustrator was advised by a former president of the Cartoonist Club of Great Britain that he would never achieve a level of ability in cartooning until he had engaged in politics. Returning to Australia, and after many yearly attempts, eventually Stonie was accepted into Rupert Murdoch's Adelaide afternoon newspaper, The News in 1984. Motor sport still followed the cartoonist. In 1984 the City of Adelaide announced it would host a round of the Formula One World Championship around the city's parkland streets. After eight years of politics and motor writing, the cartoonist-come-writer was freelance again because Murdoch closed The News in March 1992. The motoring and motor sport hub of Australia was mostly based in Melbourne. In 1996, three years after John went there to live, the Australian Grand Prix moved to Melbourne. Stoneham added media liaison to his editorial cartoon duties at many events including the Australian Grand Prix, the FIA international marathon desert rally round, the 1997 Australian Safari, and, from 1998 to 2004, an international tarmac event, the Classic Adelaide Rally. This book is the result of a serious amount of mucking about in motor cars!

John Stoneham

CLASSIC MOTOR CARTOON BOOK

AUSTIN MACAULEY PUBLISHERS™
LONDON • CAMBRIDGE • NEW YORK • SHARJAH

Copyright © John Stoneham (2020)

The right of **John Stoneham** to be identified as author of this work has been asserted by the author in accordance with section 77 and 78 of the Copyright, Designs and Patents Act 1988.

All rights reserved. No part of this publication may be reproduced, stored in a retrieval system, or transmitted in any form or by any means, electronic, mechanical, photocopying, recording, or otherwise, without the prior permission of the publishers.

Any person who commits any unauthorised act in relation to this publication may be liable to criminal prosecution and civil claims for damages.

A CIP catalogue record for this title is available from the British Library.

ISBN 9781788487283 (Paperback)
ISBN 9781788487290 (Hardback)
ISBN 9781528954747 (ePub e-book)

www.austinmacauley.com

First Published (2020)
Austin Macauley Publishers Ltd
25 Canada Square
Canary Wharf
London
E14 5LQ

PEOPLE THANKS

Sue Ellis (nee Brockbank) and
the Brockbank Family.
Angus MacKenzie,
Motor Trend Magazine (LA).
John Macdonald Automotive & Motor Sport
Industry Executive,
Sue Hardy.
Sub-editing and proofreading,
Sandy Mutton Production collaboration,
Unique Cars (Australia) Magazine.

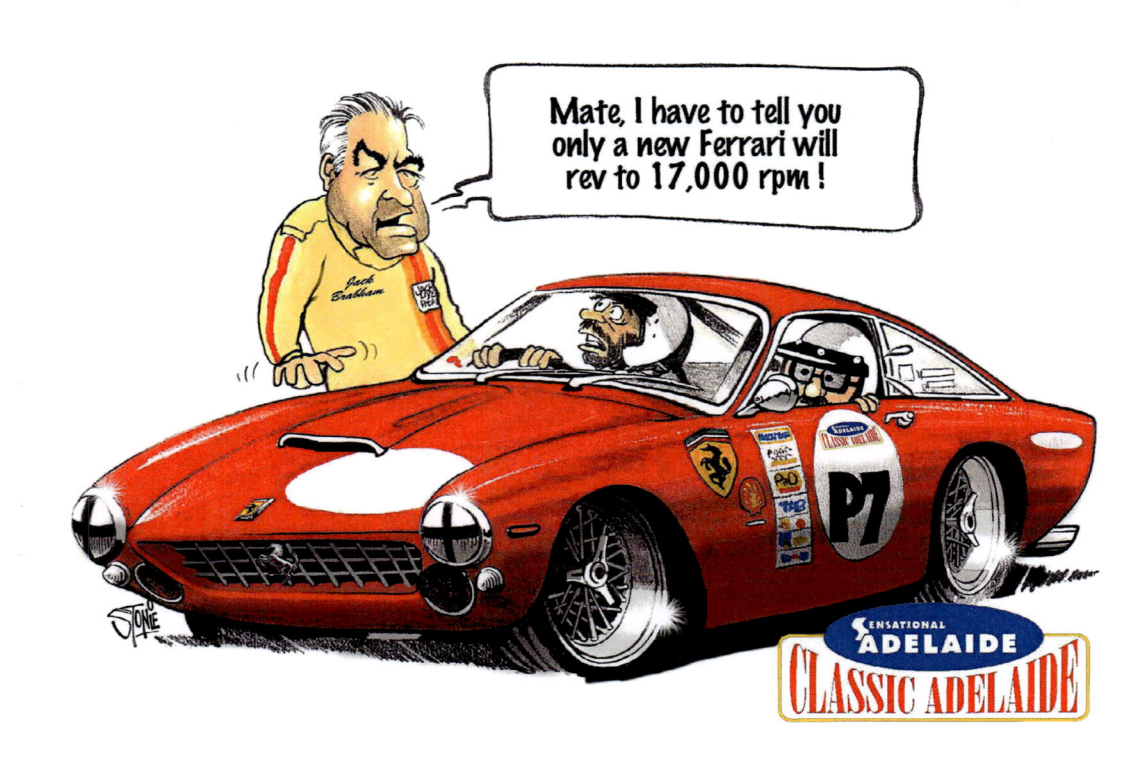

In memory of Sir Jack Brabham and his humour during the Classic Adelaide Rally.

Tribute to Russell Brockbank (1913-1979)

Every Car Club in the Western world and beyond is probably guilty of pirating a Brockbank cartoon for their in-house magazine.

We grew up in the 50s and 60s copying the black and white line work of cars drawn by this Canadian-British cartoonist motoring enthusiast.

It was instant recognition of cars in Brockbank cartoons, because with his pen work there was no mistaking a Bentley, Citroën or, famously, his Minis.

Born in Niagara Falls, Ontario Canada, Russell Partridge Brockbank moved to England in 1929 aged 26. During the Second World War Brockbank's high definition art was published in the British war training manual, Aircraft Recognition.

Totally inspired by Russell's auto illustrations, I have attempted to follow a similar style of sketching motor cars.

Meeting Russell's daughter Sue at the 2011 Goodwood Revival motor sport event was a great privilege and provided an insight into his comic vision of everything. I was told he once drove a Mini Cooper weaving through the streets of New York traffic.

John Stoneham

Veteran, Vintage, Classic
...or Just an Old Clunker?

When the Second World War finished in 1945, the automobile provided a new sense of freedom, with car designers giving us fresh rounded shapes to decorate our egos and parade a new image of ourselves.

Music also changed from the jitterbug to rock and roll, with greased-back hair and the car radio ushering in the classic era of motoring.

Pre-war cars became post-war hot rods and the obsession for the motor car accelerated with the new baby boomers, who became like Mister Toad in Wind in the Willows.

Car chase movies Bullitt, The Italian Job, James Bond 007, American Graffiti and Thelma & Louise enhanced the romance of the car. Television shows the calibre of Route 66, The Saint and Dukes of Hazzard set the scene for new trends, with the centrepiece being the automobile.

The eighties heralded the restoring and owning of a veteran, vintage or classic automobile as a sound investment, which, by the turn of the century, was climbing into a valuable asset.

Classic car collectors justified their obsession with the automobile by their wanting to re-live a wasted youth or finding and restoring their dad's car they first learnt to drive. Another validation was buying back and restoring the car in the back seat of which they first experienced the facts of life!

Old vintage and classic cars are not pretentious; a gleaming restored Triumph Herald will turn heads where a new Ferrari won't even raise an eyebrow.

With the looming inevitability of electric cars, the fascination for the motor car as we know it today will no doubt eventually be crushed, buried and dissolved into humorous folklore, be it veteran, vintage, classic or just an old clunker!

Angus MacKenzie, international editor for Motor Trend in Los Angeles, captures the spirit of classic motoring with his famous line: "Old cars are fun to drive as long as you have nowhere to go and all day to get there."

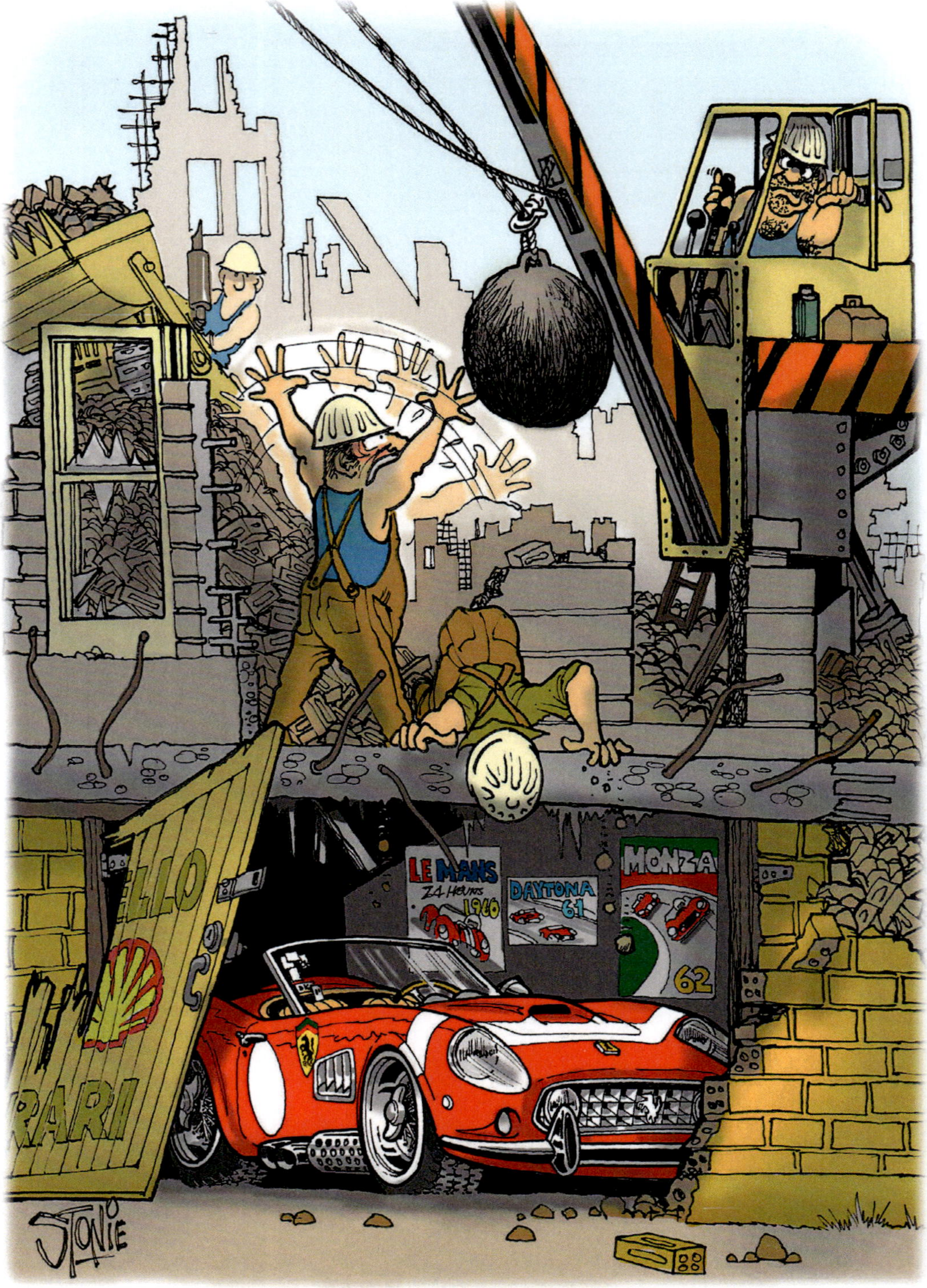
LE MANS
24 HEURES
1960
DAYTONA
61
MONZA
62
LLO
RARI
STONIE

Sorry about the smell !
Quite all right, I thought it was the car !
VEGETABLE OILS
DS
Digby Special
SA 6
STONIE

CAR CLUBS
CAR RALLIES
CAR PEOPLE

No, we're not a club. We only drive with people we like !
TRUMPIE
STONIE

PUB
PERTH
KUNU-BLOODY-NURRA
BENTLEYS ROUND OZ
Why would I ever get something with such rediculously skinny wheels like that for out here ?
Because we're bogged and HE'S NOT!
RULE BRIT
STONIE
UC #255

BUGGER !
Bloody Hell Bert, what sort of instruction is... "Right-5...Oh Shit-Trees" ?
RALLY
STONIE

BIRD WORLD
EAGLES
CHOOKS
PARROTS
FINCHES
MAGPIES
OPEN
10-4
$10
BIRDWOOD...
DAPHNE.
BIRDWOOD!
STONIE
3170
BAY TO BIRDWOOD RALLY
CLASSIC
JCC
JAG·100

1936 Aston Martin Le Mans 2 litre

The British manufacturer Aston Martin always designed their sports cars for the cavalier racing driver type and when they got it right, the cars were stunning. Even to modern eyes, this car's proportions are perfection.

Lionel Martin founded the company in 1913 and competed in his creation at the Aston Clinton hillclimb near London, thus the name Aston Martin.

With a bit of a gap while the world was at war, the next model didn't appear until 1922.

It was designed to beat speed records around the banked oval at Brooklands, England despite a small 1.5-litre engine that nicely flicked the chassis around the cement at 122mph.

In 1927, Aston Martin produced a very advanced overhead-camshaft engine and won the Biennial Cup at the 1932 Le Mans 24-Hour race, and then did it again in 1935.

The 1936 Le Mans version did not race that year because the French 24-hour event was cancelled.

Tractor manufacturer David Brown purchased Aston Martin in 1947 and from then on all models carried his initials DB before the model number.

ASTON MARTIN LE MANS 2 LITRE 1936

How long before we might have a left drive shaft for a 911 RS ?
Umm , about ten minutes !
INSTANT MIDDAY TARGA SPARES
TARGA TASMANIA
STONIE

PURPLE PORSCHE 930 ...NUMBER 376?
YEP!
...SAME CORNER AS LAST YEAR!
STONIE

Ummmm ... I think our Drinking T... Team has a Rally problem !
OFFICIAL
CAR 71
1951 WINE RALLYE
ROUTE CHART
STONIE

Did you get the size of THOSE ?
Yep...about 56D !
377
XKD 605
STONIE

1938 MG Keller SA Type 2.3 litre Straight 6

Morris Garages (MG) are best known for their two-seater, record-breaking time trials and their motor sport winning four-cylinder sports cars. MG would become a giant in performance light cars and motor racing, but started in the saloon market modifying Morris Oxfords and Cowleys in the mid-twenties.

They became an elite member of the few carmakers with initials as the brand emblem. Formed as a competition department of the William Morris group, its general manager, Cecil Kimber, is accredited with initiating the MG badge within the famous octagon. What was to become the traditional MG grille first appeared on the Mark I by the thirties, at which time the speed model competed in the 1931 Monte Carlo Rally.

Fast-forward through the TA MG series to the pre Second World War and the 1938 SA Type 2.3-litre straight six was almost a Jaguar SS copy.

Keller coach builders of Switzerland styled models based on the SA type which resembled a Mercedes-Benz staff car. Other coach builders like Tickford also styled the WA Type MG. However these models did not seem to fit the MG brand and the world war killed off the big MGs which are quite collectable today.

HEY, Your car is a ROLLER!
Actually it's a 1938 Keller SA Type MG!
2008 RALLYE MG
271
STONIE

1948 Ford Tudor Coupe V8 'Single Spinner'

During World War II all auto makers held off production and stayed with their pre-war models but the celebrations of war's end revitalised the imagination of auto designers.

The first post-war Ford off the line was known as the Shoebox design, moving away from the previous bulbous Rorty Forties. The Tudor V8 Coupe captured the market mood with its distinctive bullet nose grille, which other markets called a spinner. In the southern hemisphere the Tudor was badged a Ford Custom.

Perhaps everyone had had enough of bullets by 1949, but oddly the spinner tag didn't apply until Ford brought out the 1951 twin spinner. Then the single spinner retrospectively got its nickname. The twin bullet nose was the forerunner of the Customline style.

The Tudor came with two engines, a 90hp straight six and the Hoorah Henry flathead 100hp V8 which won the popularity stakes hands down. A "woody" estate wagon was in the range too, and Ford Australia fabricated the two-door model into impressive ambulance and panel van specials.

It was capable of 100mph on long, dusty Australian outback roads, but Ford would soon learn that Aussie remote country driving required a car that would not make occupants seasick from soft suspension or rattle itself to pieces.

Post-war Ford fans became very vocal and passionate about the blue oval. Ford reigned supreme in the American NASCAR racing code.

In Australian saloon car racing a war-like situation developed between Ford and the General Motors-Holden cars. The Tudor Ford was the start of the huge American muscle car industry!

A little Ford Company yarn suggests that "Tudor" stands for "two-door" in American Ford-speak, which means a "Fordor" is a standard saloon. No, it is not April Fool's Day!

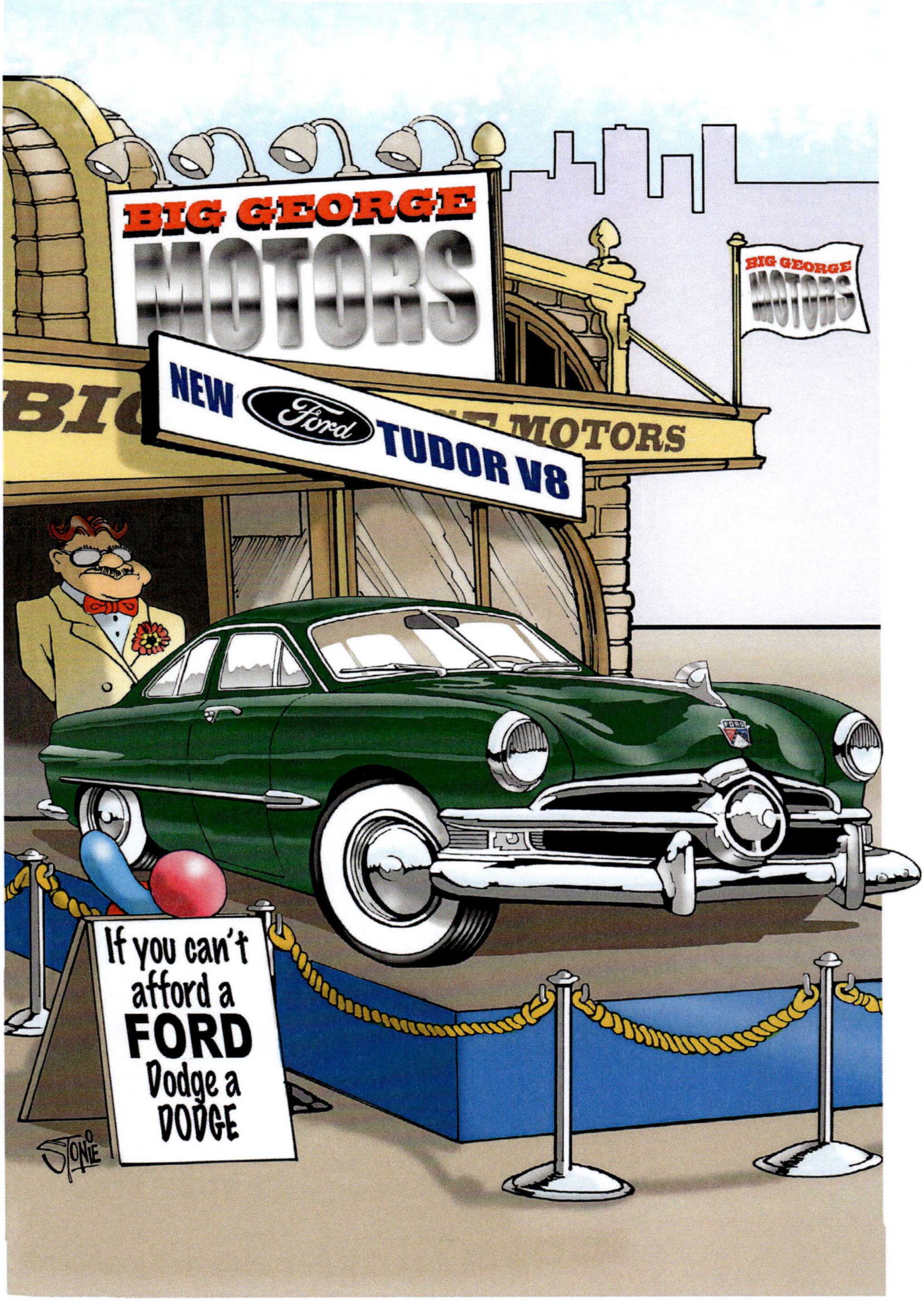
BIG GEORGE
MOTORS
NEW Ford TUDOR V8
BIG GEORGE
MOTORS
If you can't afford a FORD Dodge a DODGE
STONIE

KHYBER PASS
BOMBAY
WHO'S WINNING THE CRICKET ?
DAILY TELEGRAPH
LONDON TO SYDNEY RALLY
312
STONIE

BOOM VROOM BO
BOOM VROOM
BOOM VROOM
BOOM VROOM
BOOMVROOM
OOMVR
BLAT BLAT BLAT BLAT BLAT BLAT BLAT BLAT BLAT
STONIE

Look at that, curvaceous body, huge rear end, chrome everywhere, bulbous bumpers, floppy upholstery, loud-gawdy paint and will make a dent in your wallet!
...Just like her car!
ROUTE 66
CAFE
THE ATTENDANT HAS A GUN
YANKGAS
YANKGAS
GAS
BUICK
DARLEN
STONIE

1968 Brabham-Torana, 79bhp twin Strommies, 120,000 miles, original wide tyres, gotta be worth at least $50K... wadda ya say?
I was so happy in Ladies' shoes.
CLASSICS
SL
BRABHAM
Torana
STONIE

Man, I gotta say...driftin' though that last corner at 120 miles per hour in this 427 mother...I am not alone in my underpants !!
Yes Sir, and when you read this you will have a major relapse !
POLICE
POLICE
POLICE
STONIE

YOU SAY IT LOOKS LIKE THE MAYFLOWER, YOU MEAN THE SHIP?
NO, I MEAN THAT ANGULAR BOX THING, THE TRIUMPH MAYFLOWER!
By wanting 'FINS' on one's conveyance, is Sir looking for some sort of Umm... "ROCKET, SURFBOARD, AIR PLANE OR FISH" ?
THE NEW CTS 3.6 V6 CADILLAC
STONIE

OLD
WIVES
TALES

Well lookie here CEDRIC ! A Drab, Ugly...Boring Car lacking Performance Named after YOU !
I got some Bad News for you too GLORIA !
Gloria

I always said while he was racing, this Mini was going to be my new Lounge suite when he retired !
SELFISH Racing
DUNLOP

Do you recall the days we spent in the back seat of my FX Holden and we had sex 'til I was senseless ?
I do, and what a good job you did on yourself !
HOLDEN
48-215
60TH
ANNIVERSARY

1938-49 Ford Prefect

Ford England began building a new four-door model in 1938, naming it the Prefect, to distinguish it from the two-door Anglia. The 1172cc sidevalve engine had an interesting water pump system that did not retard horsepower from the fan, yet still kept the engine cool.

It wasn't the British summer it needed to be protected from, as the windscreen wipers had a vacuum system operated from the engine manifold.

If you were going uphill in the rain and switched on the windscreen wipers, the engine would throw in the towel and the car would roll backwards because of the drop in manifold pressure, while the wipers stopped, rendering vision impossible.

The Prefect deluxe version grille was wonderfully attractive...and Ford UK used an almost identical grille on its famous big brother, the 1947 Ford Pilot saloon with its small 2.2-litre sidevalve V8 engine.

1949 FORD AUSTRALIA PREFECT

1967 Triumph TR5 PI – TR250

Giovanni Michelotti's lovely body design of the Triumph TR4 carried over nicely to the hot rod 1967-68 TR5. Triumph claimed the TR5 was the first fuel-injected car in Britain. That innovation, combined with a gutsy 2.5-litre straight six engine and 72-spoke wire wheels, firmly targeted buyers in the market who couldn't do the E-Type Jaguar thing.

Triumph always liked to produce product models to appeal to the lucrative American market, starting with the TR2 and TR3. Now with this big-six TR5, it seemed to appeal to the Americans over the big Austin Healeys.

Ironically the advanced fuel injection was stopped at the wharf in the USA because of emission standards. A carburetted version TR250, with the Triumph horizontal bonnet racing stripe, featured twin carburettors.

Another Triumph attribute was the carry-over surrey top from the TR4. This was a great safety point and the weatherproof fixed rear window frame, on the back quarters behind the cabin, came with a centre fabric cover over the cockpit... á la surrey top!

Porsche used the same idea for the 911 and 914 models but used a hard removable roof centrepiece that could be stored in the front bonnet compartment. This unique model style was called a "Targa" which is Italian for "plate" thus, allegedly, the Porsche Targa was born.

The TR5 was the prettiest Trumpie and had a short production run which makes it a desirable classic. It was an interim model, while Triumph tooled up for the new TR6.

1968 Triumph TR5   1950 Fergusion TE20

1954 Buick Wildcat II Concept Car

Carmakers love to shock the automobile industry at Motor Shows with a concept car and Buick went out of this world with the 1954 Wildcat II at the General Motors Motorama car show in New York that year.

Chief designer at Buick, Ned Nichols, with healthy influence from design director, Harley Earl, built this prototype using a fibreglass body on polished-metal inner fenders. The signature Buick bonnet portholes on the side of the hood were the finishing touch.

The radical open-front wheel design and massive chrome front bumpers certainly would have been a customer magnet if it had gone into production, but it never did.

It now sits in the Sloan Museum Buick Gallery in Michigan. However, an automobile fanatic and self-confessed Buick nut, Ken Mitson, went on a mission from God to build a one-off replica, down to the original metal, flake blue duco. It took Ken Mitson eight years with the co-operation of Buick to complete the one and only road-going Buick Wildcat II.

1954 BUICK WILDCAT

1960-63 Chevrolet Corvair

Jack Brabham (later Sir Jack) won the Formula One World Championship in 1959 with a rear-engined Cooper race car. He was also the first man to race a rear-engined car at the Indianapolis 500.

General Motors designer and later Chief of GM, Ed Cole, had already come up with a flat-six alloy rear-engined project called the Corvair, rumoured to be a name partly Corvette and partly Bel Air.

This radical American automobile design would cause not only a tidal wave of controversy in America but the ripples would go all the way to Germany. Ralph Nader wrote a book *Unsafe at Any Speed* targeting the well-known unusual handling responses of not only the Corvair rear-engined flat-six design, but also those evident in Germany's Beetle "peoples' wagons".

Nader exposed the decision by GM bean counters not to include a front end stabiliser bar on the production Corvairs. The Oversteer threw the back-end into the trees at speed. The consequences were serious for drivers if they got the handling wrong.

GM decisively fixed the original front-end problem on the second generation model and the Corvair continued to walk out of the showrooms. The Monza versions were credited with 26,000 units sold in the first two days of going on sale.

In 1972 the Texas AM University concluded that the 1960-63 Corvair was no worse than any of its competitors in the industry (not very flattering to our American friends' motor cars). However ex-GM executive John Z. De Lorean said in his book *On a Clear Day You Can See General Motors*, "Ralf Nader was right!"

1964 CHEV CORVAIR MONZA "TOPLESS"

1957 Ford Mercury Turnpike V8

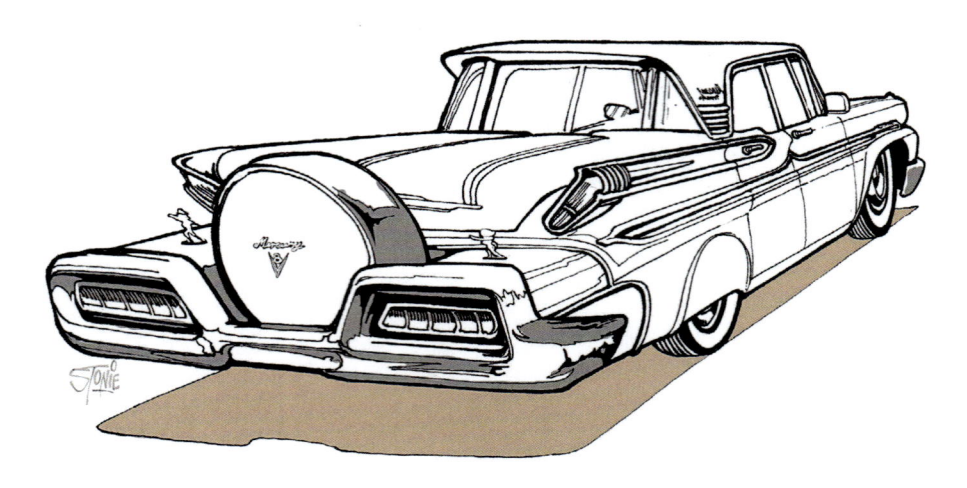

American cars never fail to astound and the 1957 Ford Mercury Turnpike V8 Hardtop takes the award as the 'Big Ass American'.

Turnpike is American for tollgate or tollway. Well, the rear end is nearly as big as a tollway and appears to be a "pull-out" drawer to hold the spare wheel without taking up space in the trunk compartment (the boot).

One of the interesting positives of the Turnpike was it had an average-speed computer in 1957... a tachometer and an opening power-assisted rear window named a "breezeway" as well. Also, to go with the American Constitution protection of personal freedoms...seat belts were an option only.

A special convertible was built as a pace car for the 1957 Indianapolis 500. Later a production version of the Indianapolis convertible came with special Continental gold-fleck tires (tyres)... only in America!

The Mercury brand was to Ford what Pontiac and Buick were to Chevrolet. The 1967 Mercury Cougar was the last interesting model; Ford put the Mercury division to sleep in 2010.

FORD MERCURY TURNPIKE V8

I've got traffic sensing control, accelerator restrictor, lane change indicator, voice warning system...all in the "Air bag" sitting alongside me!
POLICE
STONIE

Serve you right for ordering the big Cudlee breakfast!
CUDLEE CAFÉ
STONIE

ONE HUNDRED YEARS OF THE VERY GENERAL MOTORS AND OTHER "THINGS"
DELOREAN –V6
DMC-2
Lotus backbone chassis, 2.8 litre V6 rear engine, Gull wing doors, ...so "Back to the Future" they will make a movie about it !
You must be on something!
FIREBIRD I
STONIE

YELSGNIK MOTORS
TRABANT DEALER
ORDER NOW!
Comrade, your Trabbie will arrive on Friday April 26, six years from now !
Is nice ! That is same day as the Gas will be connected !
STONIE

1957 Jaguar XK 140

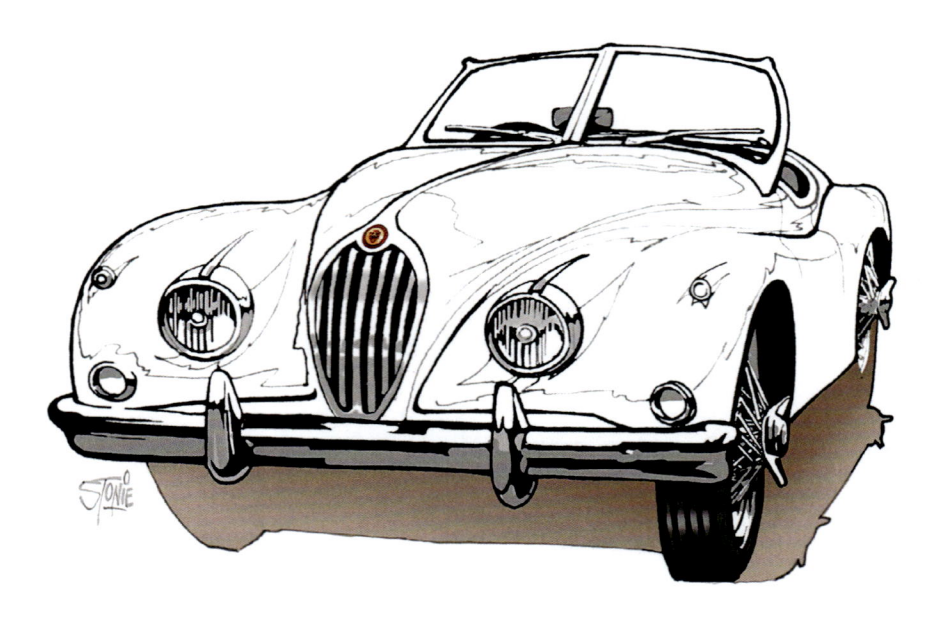

Sitting in the air raid shelters during the Battle of Britain, William Lyons (later Sir William Lyons) was penning his ideas to revitalise the Jaguar Car Company for when the noise stopped and everyone went back to work. Old Bill had a definite post-war dream to make Jaguar the best of British in the car industry.

The result was a very durable and long-lasting XK engine and thank the Lord, he went with the twin-cam version. Some car companies make laughable mistakes by giving their cars pet-names; not Jaguar, the name is "Jaguar" and the rest of the badge is letters and numbers.

Jaguar nuts will argue to the death about which are the best XK models and all have their own story. The XK 120 was the first of the modern roadsters and probably the fastest. The XK140 with its less expensive cast-iron seven-bar grille, wire wheels and American standard bumpers gave the middle-class enthusiasts just the car they wanted back in the day. It also gave Americans a production Jaguar.

With a slightly lower production run of 8,800, some collectors today say the XK140 is nice to have if you were canny enough to pick one up in the seventies for a nice little "dollar".

The XK "120" was an indication of its mph top speed...not so much the "140" or the "150"! Has anyone noticed: it's a Jaguar created by Lyons!

When he ran off with his secretary, his last words were...get a good dollar for my old Jaguar! "Yeah, this looks like a good one!"
FOR SALE $1
18
STONIE

1948 Morris Minor MM Series Lowlight

Alec Issigonis (later Sir Alec), was the designer who gave Britain its first post-war people's car when it most needed it. The working class made it the first million-seller in Britain.

The Morrie Minors kept selling until 1969 with an upgrade from the lowlight to the Highlights, all with convertible models right up to the lovable Morris Minor 1000.

During the war there was a ban on local car production in England, but the Nuffield engineers wanted to be ready with a new car after the war ended. The original designs were called the Mosquito project.

Lord Nuffield didn't like the name Mosquito or the initial designs, and went so far as to say he didn't approve of Issigonis that much either! He called the look of the new car a "bloody poached egg"!

The new small British car went from a Mosquito to a Minor and was duly launched at the 1948 Earl's Court Motor Show.

The rack-and-pinion steering and independent front suspension made the underpowered 918cc side-valve-engined Minor great fun to drive. Rumour has it Stirling Moss lost his licence skylarking around in a Morrie. The policeman asked him... "Who do you think you are, Stirling Moss?"

Of course Alec Issigonis went on to design the world's most famous small car, the Mini. However sales of the Morris Minor continued after the Mini was released.

1948 MORRIS MINOR MM SERIES LOWLIGHT

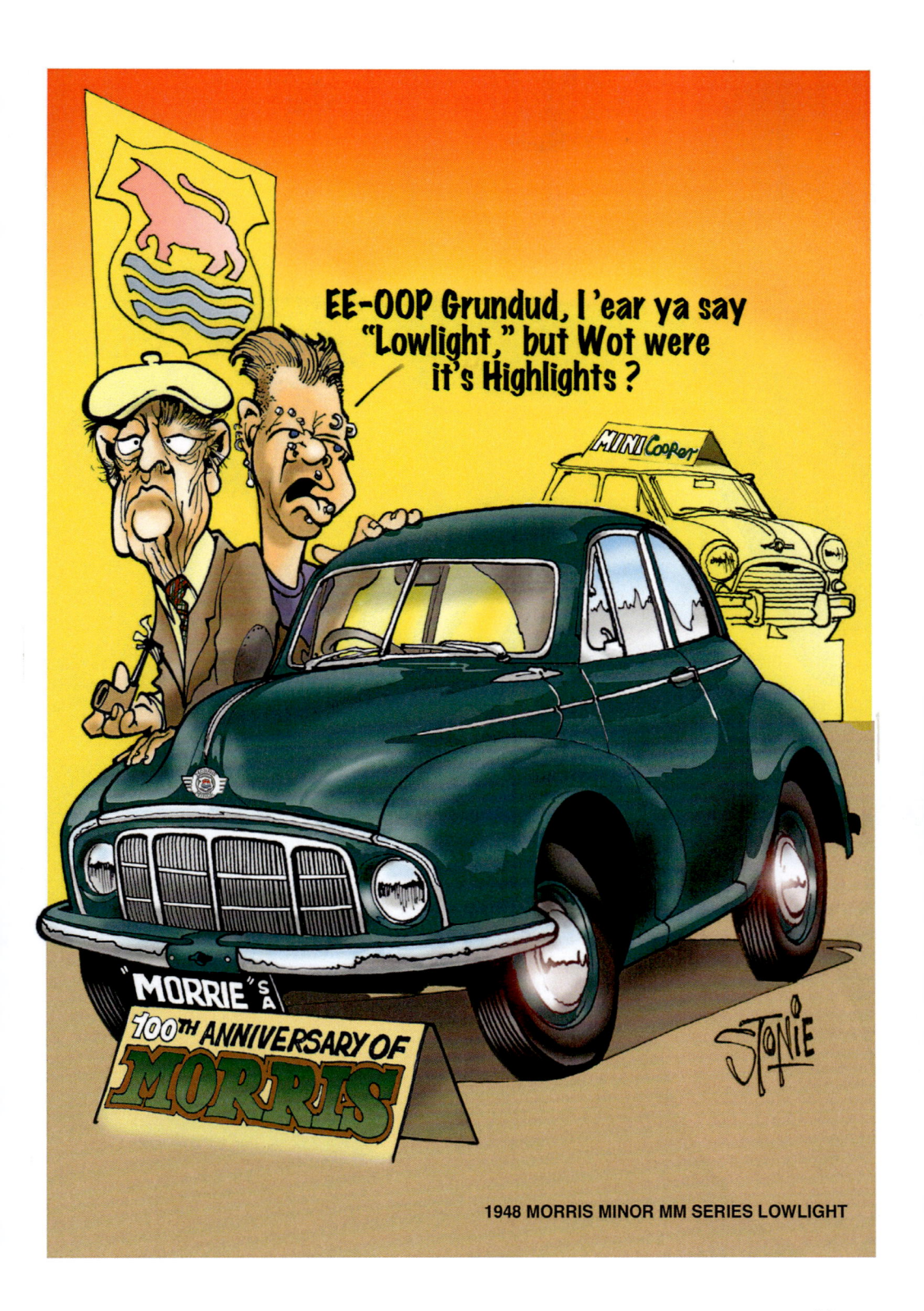

1967-68 Pontiac Firebird

Pontiac, Michigan is named after the local Ottawa Native American war chief; General Motors also named their new 1926 vehicle manufacturing plant after him.

As a diversion away from Pontiac's mid-sized stable of cars, one young turk at GM (soon to be famous), John Z. De Lorean, was keen to produce cars aimed at the young adult market. After the controversial Corvair Monza, De Lorean launched the more traditional and larger first Pontiac GTO in the same year as the famous Ford Mustang, 1964.

The Mustang, in its hipster coke-bottle body shape of the era, was joined by the Pontiac Firebird, launched in 1967, both referred to as pony cars.

While the Ford Mustang was the rock star of the US market, this new Pontiac Firebird was the unique underdog. It offered a similar six-cylinder starter package to the Mustang at first, but options of four big V8 engines highlighted the theme De Lorean wanted for the youth market.

The Firebird was always the kid brother to the GTO and struggled with sales against the Mustang. Today, however, in the classic American car market, the huge chrome integrated front bumper with its pointed beak nose and signature GTO bonnet nostrils is a discerning choice versus the Mustang.

Also, due to the low production run in both the coupe and convertible versions, the 1967-69 Firebird certainly should be a worthy investment. Pontiac's idea of an optional tachometer mounted outside of the cabin on the bonnet is a plus when looking for a Firebird to buy. Also note that the door-mounted quarter vents disappeared from the 1968 model.

1968 Pontiac Firebird

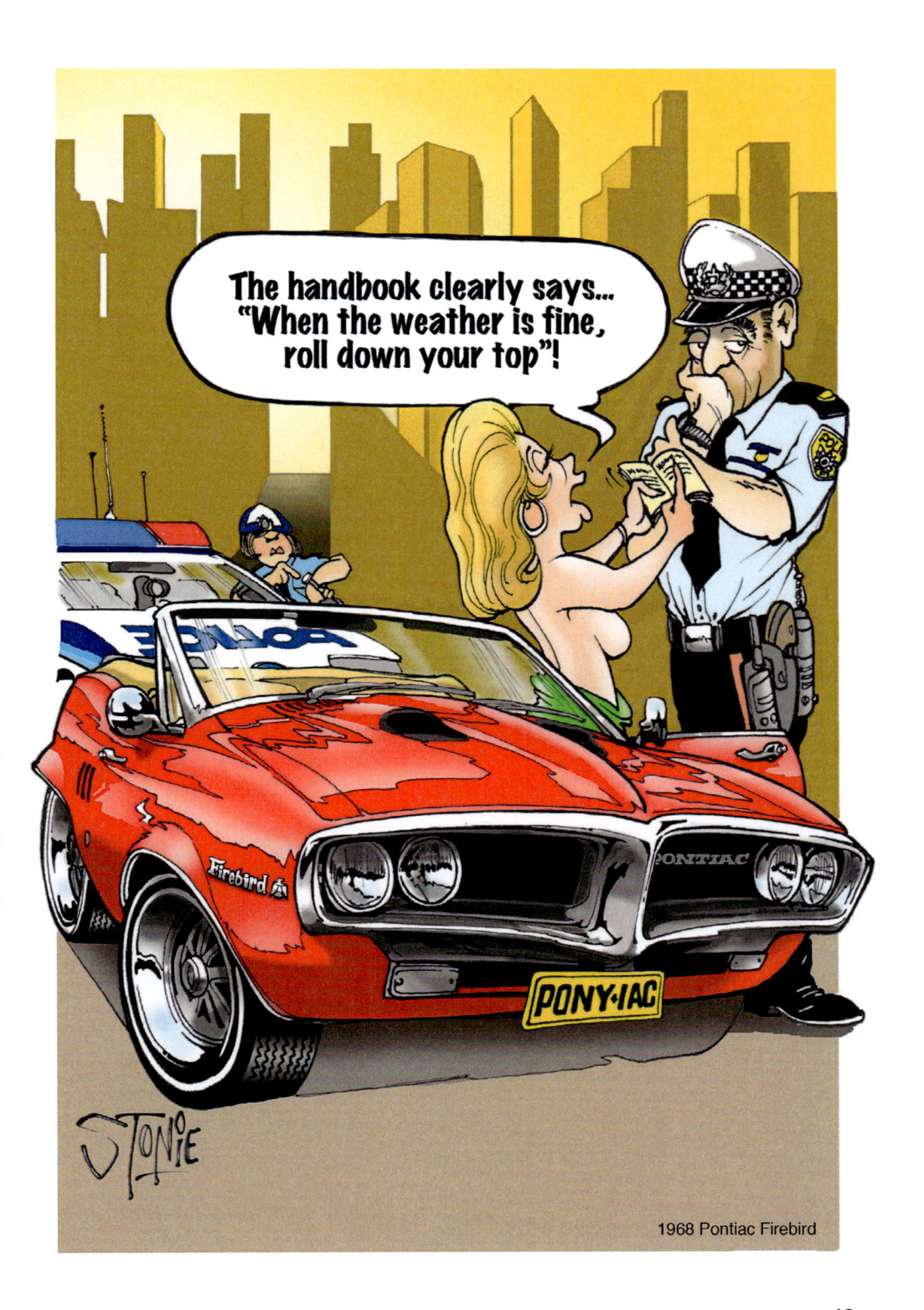

1958 Nash Rambler Metropolitan

If ever an American automobile company seemed to go the wrong way down the model road you might think the Nash company did with the Nash Rambler Metropolitan, later to become a Hudson.

This little grandma car copped the brunt of automobile jokes as a pumped-up economy job to look like a big-little car that resembled an up-turned bathtub! Its Austin UK-based 1200cc engine and three-speed transmission made it impossible to keep pace with American muscle car iron of the day.

As motoring writers overcame their belief that it wouldn't pull a sailor off your sister, the Metropolitan's economy and gentle speed swayed their objections.

A pop song was even written about the Nash Rambler's agility, recorded by the Playmates in 1958...*Beep Beep* became the theme song for all small cars around the world. The lyrics portrayed the Nash chasing a Cadillac down the highway constantly beeping its horn to pass. Reaching speeds that were way over the legal limit the song says the Nash Rambler pulled up alongside the Caddie and asked... *"How do you get this car out of second gear?" song lyrics.*

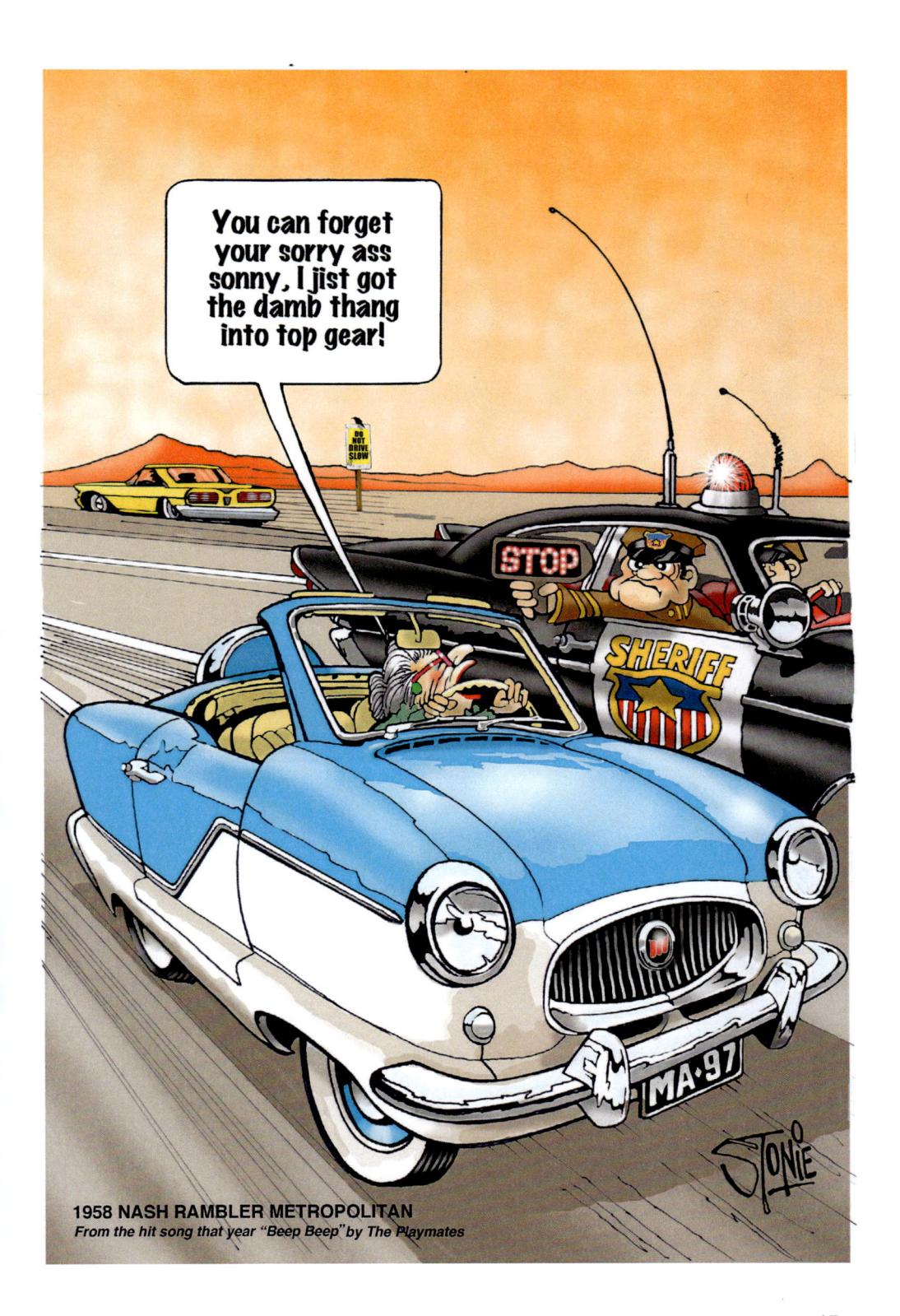

1958 NASH RAMBLER METROPOLITAN
From the hit song that year "Beep Beep" by The Playmates

1951 Studebaker Commander "Bullet Nose"

From behind, the split-screen back window of the Studebaker Commander bullet nose saloon made it look like it was going backwards. It became known as the "push-me-pull-you" car after the Doctor Dolittle beast.

The Commander Studey also had a cabin with both rear doors opening out in opposite directions making easy entry into the rear passenger area. The back-opening suicide doors never really became popular, probably a safety concern of what might happen if they were opened in motion! It's interesting that the current Rolls-Royce has the same design.

As early settlers to the new land of America, the Stutenbecker family immigrated from Germany in 1736. The immigration officer at the arrival station in Philadelphia filled out their papers as the "Studebaker" family and so it remained.

In the beginning the family business was making horse-drawn buggies, then motorisation saw the company produce trucks. During World War II, Studebaker produced army vehicles for their now American homeland.

After the war Studebaker designed and produced the Studebaker Champion, again with its unique rear-window design. This time their vehicles were nicknamed "the coming-and-going cars".

Later Studebaker produced a huge two-door coupe with a supercharged V8 called either the Silver or Golden Hawk. It became a legend!

Why do you think Dad is having an affair?
He keeps talking about this new love in his life... a "JUDY BAKER!"
STUDEY
STONIE

A good lookin' sleeper...
not bad eh ?
Yeah, 1.6 litre, Porsche 356 donk, chrome 6" fats, Aquajets and 115 miles per hour!
STONIE

They say a man's car is an extension of his appendage !
That small eh ! What does it say about his wallet ?
Hotel Plaza
STONIE

PONTIAC
Alfa Romeo
Tony's BAR & GRILLE
Tony's
Coffee Shop
STAFF ONLY
STONIE

1968 Austin Healey MKIII 3000

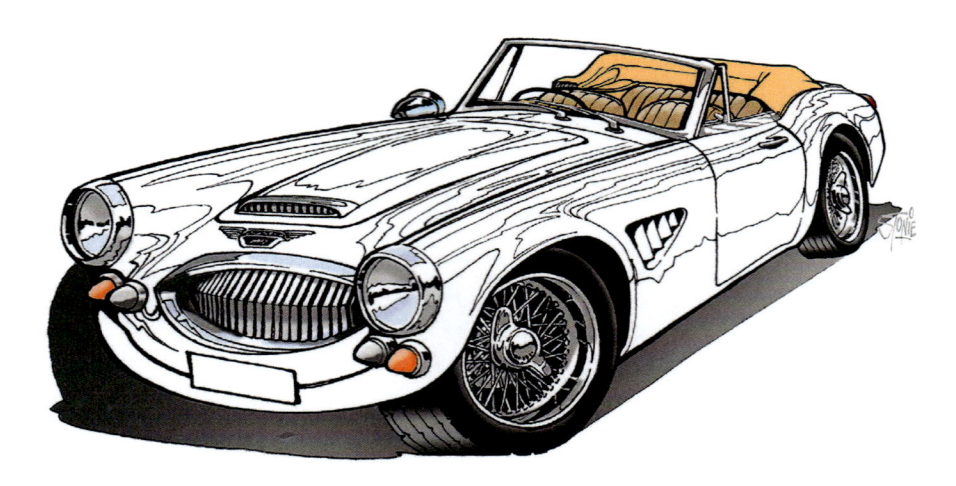

Brutal... is a good word for the Austin Healey MKIII 3000. It's heavy, fast and fortunately, has a nice long wheelbase that will glide you through any line you want to grab on tarmac or dirt surfaces.

It's hard today to imagine that iconic sports cars were used as rally cars in the mid-sixties and even more so that it was a fast lady who manhandled these monsters in the World Rally Championship arena.

Pat Moss drove a big Healey to first place in the 1960 Liegé-Rome-Liége, was second in the Coupes des Alpes in 1961 and second also at the 1962 RAC Rally.

Pat's Father was a motorsport competitor and she was taught to drive by her brother, oddly enough called Stirling.

With this good gene pool in her career DNA, Pat took three outright wins, seven international podiums and was four times Lady Rally Champion. Staying with the BMC Works Team before she moved to Ford, Pat won the Netherlands Tulip Rally in a Mini Cooper which when compared to the big Healey, Pat said was a bit twitchy and unresponsive.

Pat married Swedish Rally ace Erik Carlsson and had a family. She left a great legacy for women drivers to follow.

The first BN-1 four-cylinder drop-screen Healey is the collector's choice. The MKIII is the muscle model and anyone who has had the opportunity to drive one of these big Healeys for any major distance will know it helps if you have forearms like *Popeye*.

No daughter of mine is getting into a car like that... unless ...I get to drive it first!
6
6
HEALIUM
STONIE

1953 Bristol 404

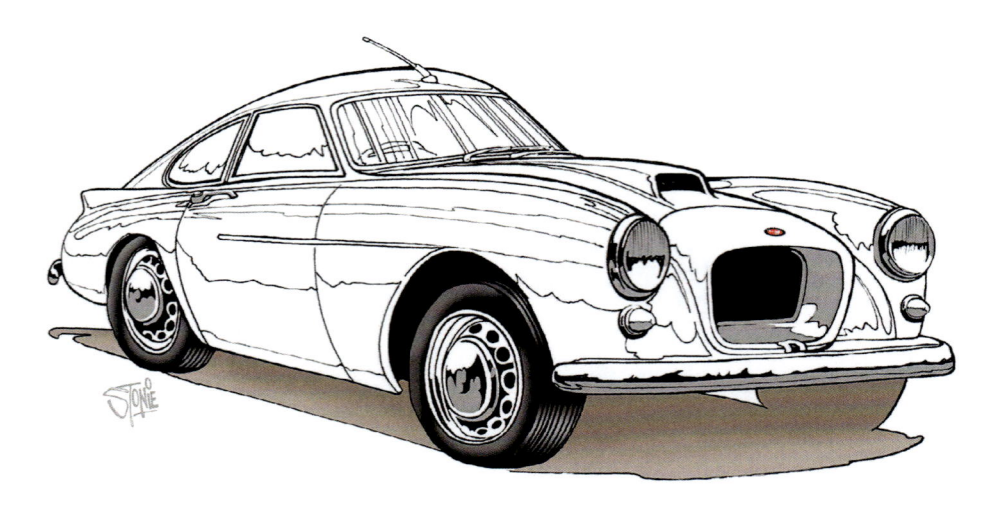

With the World Wars as a backdrop, the Bristol Aeroplane and Car Company has a great story as an amazing British manufacturer. After the First World War, the Bristol Aeroplane Company saved itself by making light cars and coach building.

With the outbreak of World War II, they launched back into the war effort employing 70,000 people manufacturing the famous Bristol aero engines. Remembering what happened after the first war, the company directors started an after-war plan as early as 1941, looking to purchase carmakers like Aston Martin, Alvis and ERA in order to maintain their huge manufacturing base.

In 1945, a chance collaboration with Frazer-Nash allowed Bristol to purchase this carmaker who oddly enough had a connection with Germany's BMW before the war. The new owners, as part of the redevelopment of Germany, went to Munich and purchased the rights to remanufacture three BMW models and use the lovely 328 engine.

As an acknowledgement of the German connection the first Bristol cars were made with BMW grille designs on the 400-401 series cars. On the later 405 Bristols they had a Lucas driving light in the middle of the grille.

Only those of us who possess the Monty Python-type humour gene will see irony in the light being affectionately nicknamed the flame thrower.

Only 53 Bristol 404 cars were ever made which makes them highly collectable.

1950 401 BRISTOL (pedestal)   1954 404 BRISTOL

1955 Rolls-Royce Dawn

You can take anyone off the street and put them into a Rolls-Royce and their personality will suddenly change. The magical multi-bar grille with the Spirit of Ecstasy bonnet emblem will open doors for anyone in a Roller.

Winston Churchill would be unimpressed these days knowing that BMW now own Rolls-Royce (Cars) and, in fact, Jaguar has been owned by the Indian company Tata Motors since 2008.

There was a Rolls-Royce fable about a French nobleman who purchased one and a year later, it broke an axle. Not overly fussed, the Frenchman wrote to Rolls-Royce requesting a replacement part for his model Roller. Some time later two men in white coats presented themselves on the Frenchman's doorstep as engineers, assigned to fix the customer's alleged problem. About two months later the Frenchman wrote to Rolls-Royce requesting an invoice for the replacement of the broken axle. The reply explained to the owner that he must be mistaken, Rolls-Royce cars don't break axles.

1955 SILVER DAWN ROLLS-ROYCE

1938 Alfa Romeo 8C Superleggera

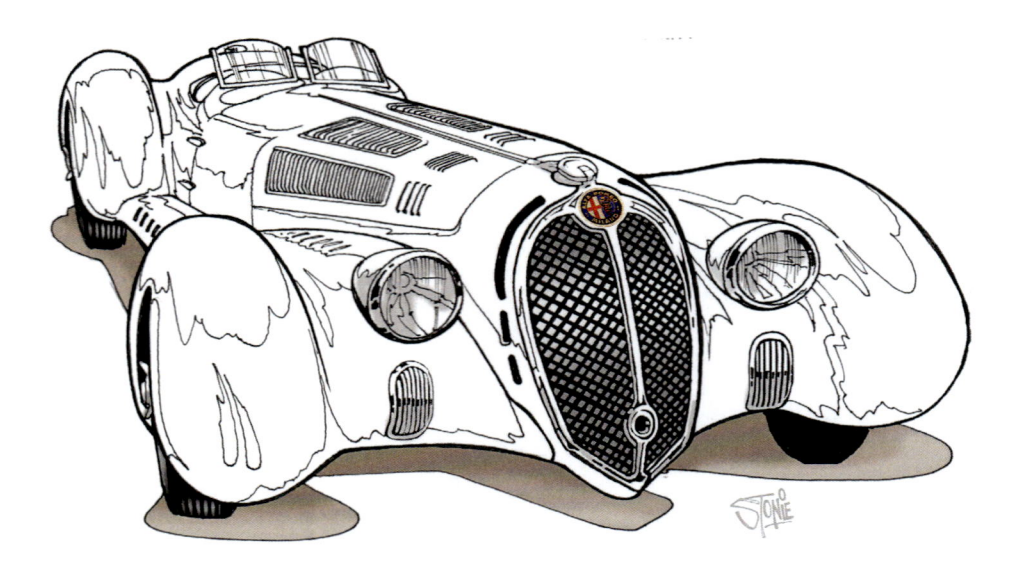

Alfa Corse was the racing department of the famous Alfa Romeo marque which built the historic pre-war Grand Prix cars. These overhead-cam straight-eight Monzas and Monopostos were the cars that a young Enzo Ferrari ran as an unofficial Alfa Romeo racing team.

In events like British TT races, the French Le Mans 24-Hour Race and the wild Italian road races such as the famous Targa Florio and Mille Miglia, these special Alfas were engineered just to win. Famous Italian body designers like Zagato, Pininfarina and Carrozzeria Touring were lining up to style the bodywork.

For the 1938 Mille Miglia, Alfa Corse built four cars for the road race and Carrozzeria Touring designed the wild and wonderful Superleggera (superlight) roadster bodies for the 8C 2900 car.

Three of the Carrozzeria cars were 225bhp-engined and the fourth had an Alfa Tipo 308 – 295bhp grand prix engine for Clemente Biondetti. He won the race and Carlo Pintacuda was second in the less powerful model.

Carrozzeria Touring techniques closed its doors in 1966 but was reborn in 2006. Alfa Romeo is associated with the Sauber Formula One Team for the 2020 season.

If you see a Carrozzeria Superleggera Alfa driving down the boulevard it will pull your eyeballs out of their sockets.

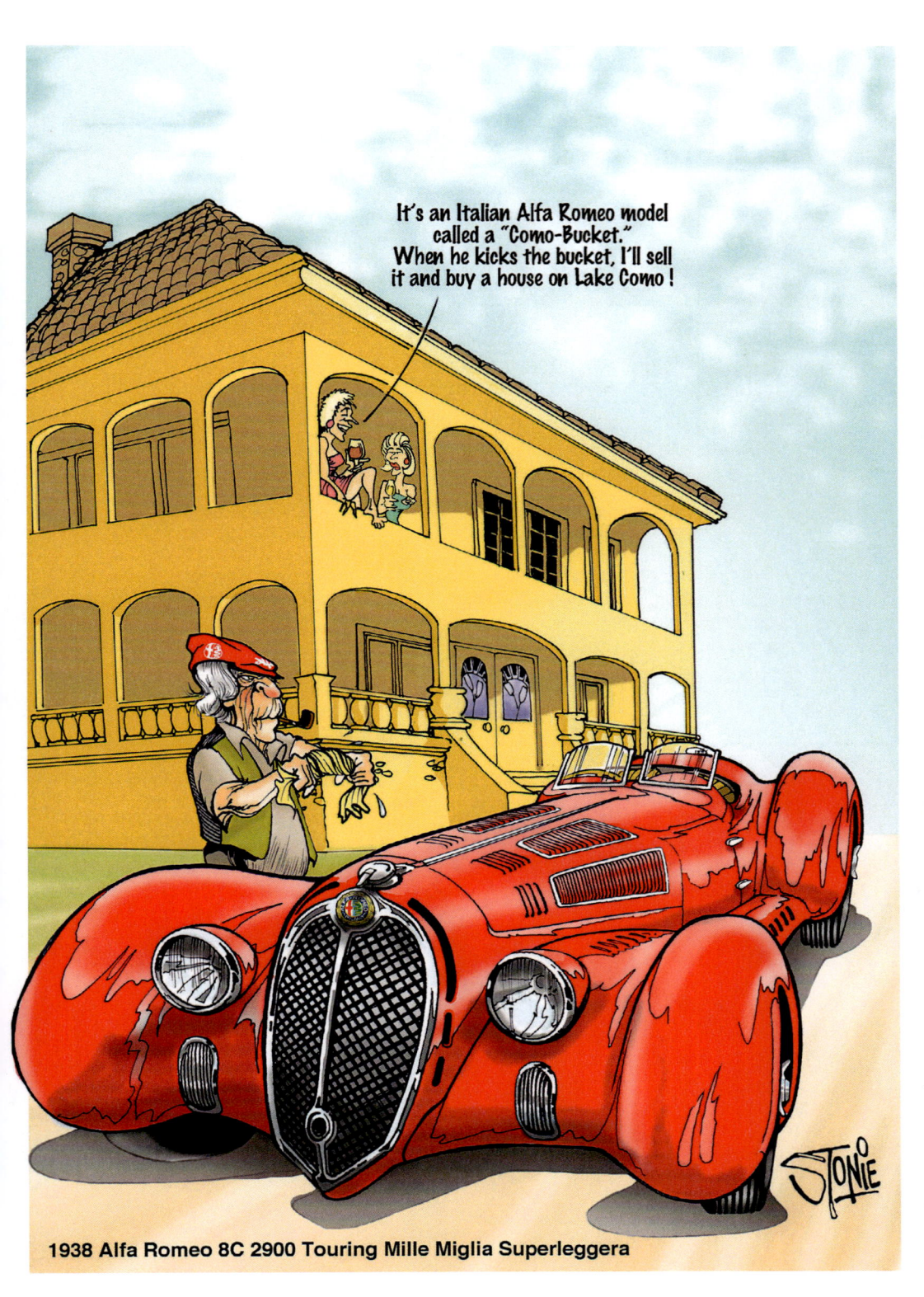

1938 Alfa Romeo 8C 2900 Touring Mille Miglia Superleggera

1960 Renault Floride Convertible

By the end of the fifties, sports models and convertibles were becoming a trend in the car market 15 years after World War II. French carmaker Renault looked hard at the success the British and German manufacturers were having with sports cars.

Then at an automobile convention in Florida, USA, Renault dealers asked the parent company for a sports model of their Dauphine saloon for the lucrative US market.

Designer Pietro Frua at Carrozzeria Ghia was charged with the task of designing a French sports job on the Dauphine Saloon floorpan with an 845cc engine. Starting with the rear-panel side air ducts, Pietro shaped a very French statement with an inset headlight touch late on a chisel nose, later copied on the MGB and the Datsun 240Z.

The new coupé and convertible, distinctively a Regie Reno, was named Floride in honour of Florida where the idea was first born. While the European market didn't mind the name when launched at the 1958 Paris Motor Show, the US Renault dealers suggested some states in the US might be peeved about the Florida badge, and thus North Americans got Renault "Caravelle"-badged cars a year after the Paris launch.

They probably thought Caravelle was a French carousel (roundabout) at a state fair. The little rear-engined 845cc in-line four later went up to 1108cc and some received a Gordini after-market performance touch. If you can find one today without rust, they make a great companion talking point.

1960 RENAULT FLORIDE DAUPHINE GORDINI 845cc

1970 Pontiac GTO "The Judge"

In the seventies everything, from fashion to automobiles, was "far out" but when Pontiac called their 1970 budget model GTO "the Judge" many noses were wrinkled in disbelief. You may not believe it, but the name came from the TV comedy show *Laugh-In* in which Flip Wilson would exclaim "Here come da Judge!". The Rowan & Martin show was a huge success in 1970 and even the GTO advertising went further with "All rise for the Judge!" and "The Judge can be bought!". Goldie Hawn made her debut on *Laugh In*.

Due to one John Z. De Lorean, the name GTO comes from the Italian for the Ferrari Stallion 250 "Gran Turismo Omologato" meaning "homologated for Grand Touring Racing". Many cars were given the GT badge to denote a high-performance model. It usually meant your car insurance policy premiums would go through the roof of the Empire State building.

Interesting that while the Ponty GTO was never raced, some models later turned up with monster engines with 6.5 and 6.9 litres for drag racing. General Motors in 1957 complied with the directive of the Automotive Manufacturers Association in America that carmakers should not race their cars as factory-backed teams. Henry Ford however ignored the directive completely.

The Pontiac GTO Judge also offered the signature external tachometer mounted on the bonnet like the Firebird, which was a "must-have" for any street-racer.

Rowan & Martin's sign-off line every night on *Laugh-In* was, "Say good night Dick," so Dick said, "Good night Dick!"

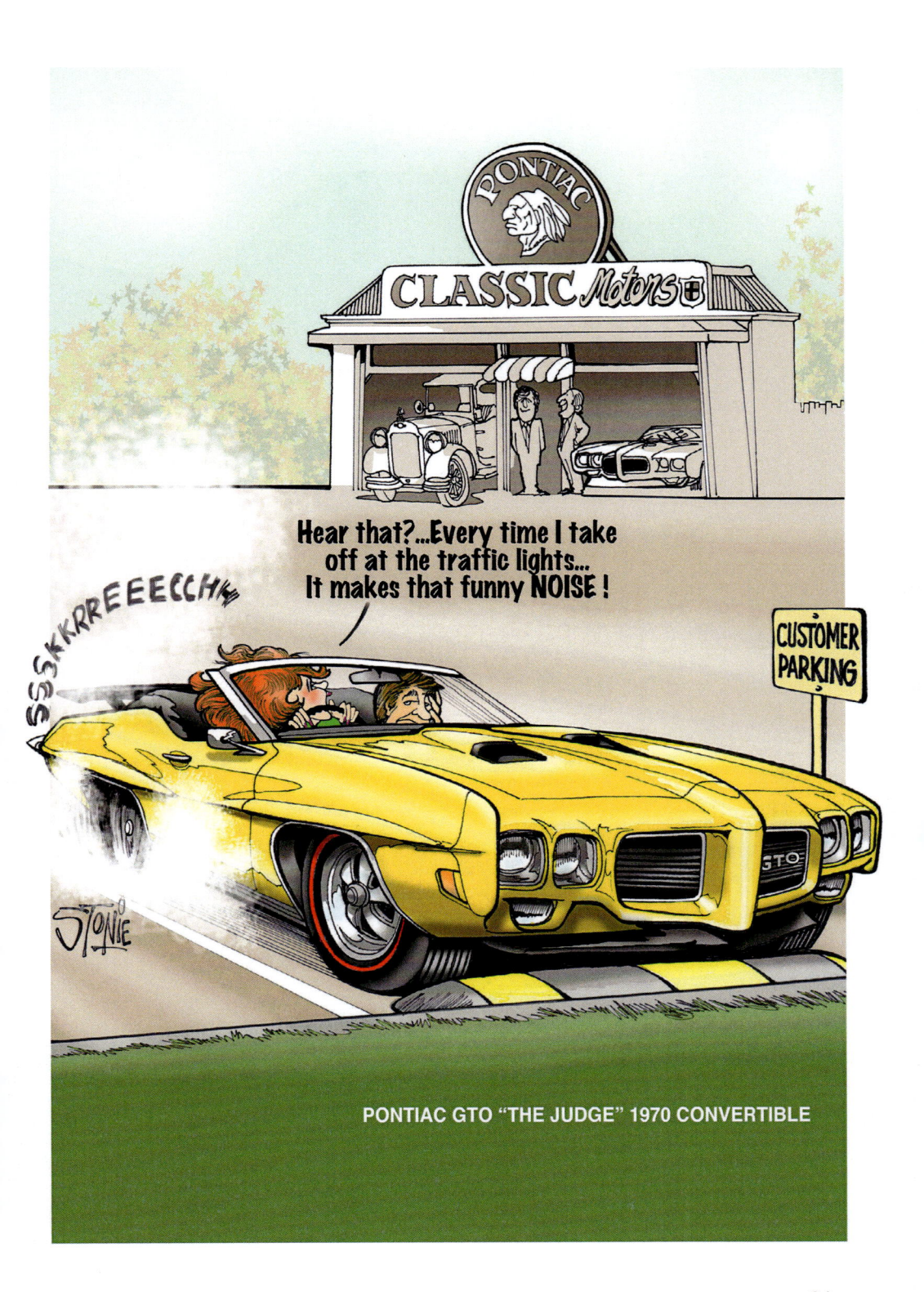

PONTIAC GTO "THE JUDGE" 1970 CONVERTIBLE

BOYS &
THEIR
TOYS

STONIE
MORGAN
BOB
TERMITES
KILLER

FORD
289
PONY-1
STONIE

Now...You wanna' see this nought-to-sixty in 8 seconds very rare "Cougar" you bought sight unseen !!
DAKOTA
HYUNDAI
CAR IMPORTS
OPEN OTHER SIDE
FEED CAREFULLY
STONIE

HULLO
Oh great ! ...If we were in the Swiss Alps, we'd be rescued by a Saint Bernard with booze on its collar. But we get a singing Swede in a SAAB !
WHOA! That ain't no Dog !
STONIE

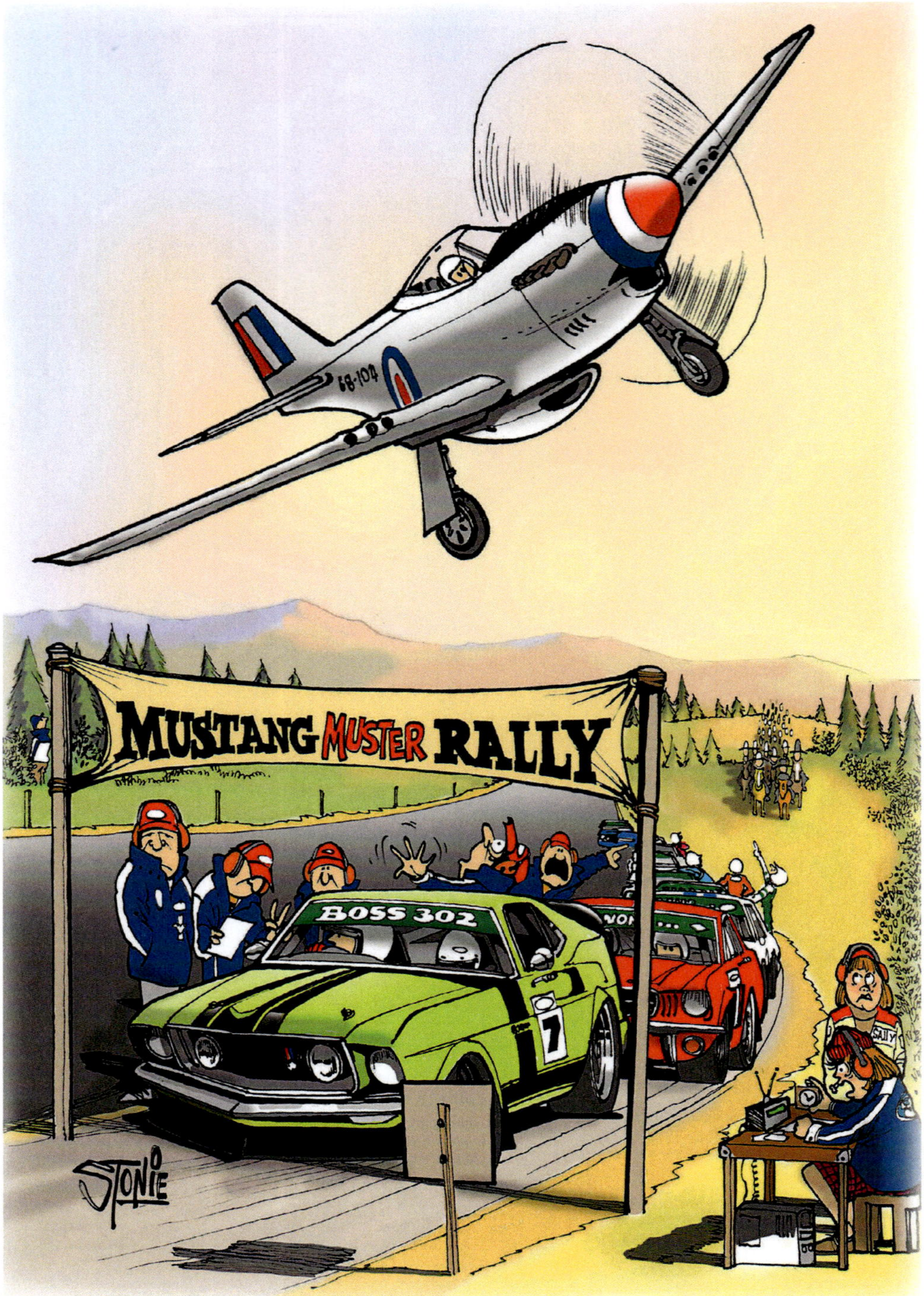

Hey, ya know the Dude I met in the bar last night who said he had a Ferrari collection... Well, you are not going to believe this !
STONIE

So Grandad, if this was your hot wheels when you were eighteen, you reckon I should hang on to my Lada Samara ?
JAG-MK2
STONIE

1966-71 GT40 Ford

Henry Ford tried to buy Ferrari, with the express purpose of winning the Le Mans 24-Hour Race. Enzo was keen to sell, but Fiat stepped in and stopped the American. Henry then called on all Ford engineers to design a Le Mans winner.

British race car builder Eric Broadley at Lola Cars had already produced a stunning design for a competitive sports-racing car with alloy bodywork. Ford US and Carrol Shelby preferred a stronger all-steel shell with a bigger 427 V8 aimed at doing 200mph.

So the GT40 was born, so named because it stood 40 inches high. Like the Spitfire War Bird, the GT40 went through a series of prototypes evolving into a real mongrel. The Mark II version won the 1966 Le Mans 24-Hour endurance race and continued to win for three more years locking Ferrari completely out of the prestigious race.

Thirty-one road versions were supposedly made of the original "Roaring Forties," and also many of the race cars were converted to road use later. If you are over six foot you may not be able to fit in a real GT40 and rumour has it six-foot American F1 driver, Dan Gurney, had bulge panels in the roof when he and stumpy A.J. Foyt won Le Mans in 1967.

Come the new millennium Ford America released a more practical version of the famous GT40...Alas they called it a Ford GT maybe because it was no longer forty inches high.

The rebirth of the GT40 Ford legend and it's racing history has been immortalised in the 2019 movie Ford vs Ferrari with some stunning racing scenes about the development of the GT40 project.

Christian Bale plays Ken Miles in the role of US race & test driver of the GT40. The Ken Miles/Denny Hulme MkII GT40 should have been accredited winner of the 1966 Le Mans race only to be robbed by a Ford executive decision to stage a 1-2-3 in-line finish rendering the leading car of Miles and Hulme to second place.

Ken Miles was killed in 1967 at Riverside Raceway testing the "J-2" (2-speed) automatic version of the GT40. There were suggestions the auto-2 speed box jammed between gears locking the back wheels and throwing car and driver off the track.

SEE YOUR TAXATION DOLLARS AT WORK
FIRST 10 LEVELS RESERVED FOR PUBLIC SERVANTS
24 HOUR VIDEO SURVEILLANCE
SEX IN CARS TAPES FOR SALE!
TOW AWAY POLICY ...FOR CAR ALARMS THAT GO OFF!!!
AUSFAHRT
OUT OF ORDER LIFTS
EXIT
THANK YOU FOR NOT DOING DRUGS
RKING
SPACES
STOP FOR TICKET
GT FORDIE
STONIE

1947-52 Austin of England A40 Devon-Dorset

Austin of England's post-war 1947 A40 was so different from the old Austin Sevens and Austin Tens with a modern rounded style and on a separate chassis. The A40 came with a modern over-head valve 1200cc engine, sitting on front coil springs, however with the old leaf spring system in the back.

The A40 came in both two- and four-door models, the Devon and the Dorset. At the 1947 Paris Motor Show, the A40 body shape was panned even though the rounded shape gave more room inside the modern bright interior.

As the Commonwealth middle classes began to prosper in the fifties, they upgraded from the likes of the Morris Minor to the more comfortable A40.

Two years later, a manufacturing arm of the Austin Company decided to make a children's toy pedal car in the shape of an open-top A40 in South Wales. This was an amazing product promotion for the A40, as the "J40" Kid's car came with pump-up tyres, working headlights, an operating horn, plus the production of the J40 ran longer than the full size A40!

The Austin A40 production run was about 450,000 and the J (for Joy) 40 were made up to 1971 with a total run today of 32,000. The original price of the J40 was £27 in 1949 and today maybe £5,000 will stop a good one. Other car models have been made into toy-pedal cars from Mercedes to Mustangs but the J40 was, and still is, the classic!

1947 Austin A40 Devon & 1949 "Junior" J40

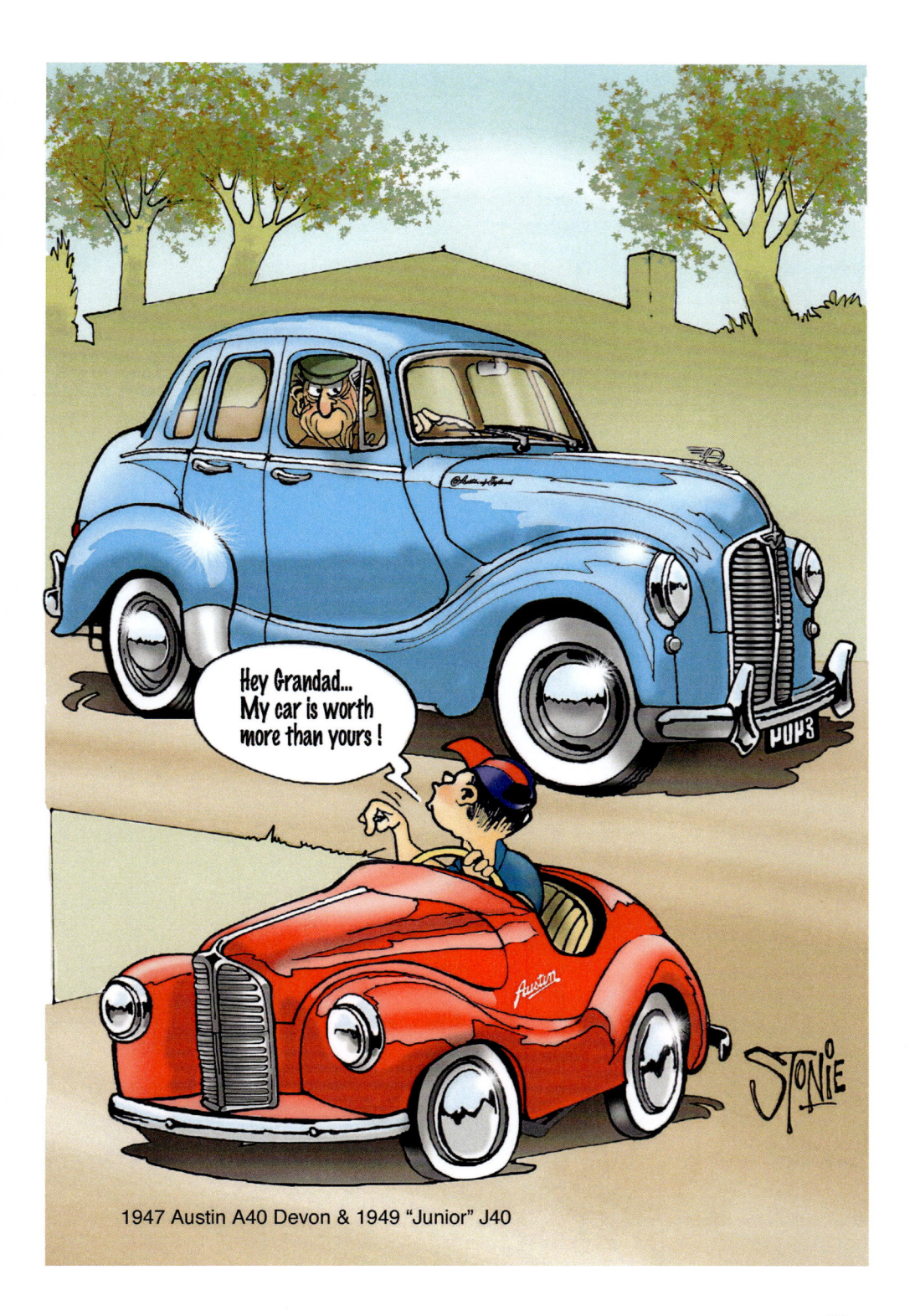

1952 Hudson Hornet Hollywood Coupe

The name is nearly as long as this famous historic monster. The Hudson Hornet has a great history competing in the early American NASCAR Series when it was held on dirt circuits. The lumbering chassis of the Hudson had a weird low-slung floor below the chassis rails, giving great low centre of gravity handling.

Hauled around by a monster five-litre six-cylinder engine labelled "twin (carbies) 145bhp H-Power", the Hornet accounted for itself with 21 NASCAR victories in the early days.

The low-cut window line two-door Hollywood Coupe was aimed and named to appeal to the in-crowd.

So what's in a name? Well, like that famous comment by pilot Captain Sully, "We're going in the Hudson!" the Hudson Hornet name (later used for the F18 strike aircraft) became a film star with a Hollywood star's voice in the animated 2006 movie Cars with the base theme of NASCAR racing.

In the movie, Lightning McQueen (presumably a homage to Steve McQueen) finds a Hudson Piston Cup NASCAR trophy in the shed of the local retired judge, Doc Hudson (a caricature of a Hudson Hornet). The voice-over was of course the film star Paul Newman. This was a nice touch in the movie as Paul privately raced sportscars as a hobby to start with and later became co-owner of the championship winning Newman/Haas Indycar team.

HUDSON HORNET HOLLYWOOD COUPE 1952 TWIN H-POWER

1953-59 The Cadillac "Big Years"

Antonine Laumet de La Mothe, sieur de Cadillac, the French explorer, founded Detroit in 1701. Acknowledging the founding Frenchman, the Cadillac Car Company was established in 1902.

General Motors bought Cadillac and the residing GM president Larry Fisher brilliantly employed the most prolific designer of General Motors American iron, Harley Earl, in 1926. Earl hired a 20-year-old apprentice Bill Mitchell in 1935.

Harley Earl loved big wings and curves, fins and fenders plus lots of chrome. This legendary car designer accepted no boundaries when it came to creating a new model and General Motors was happy to bank on Earl's reputation as a Hollywood designer.

Cadillac was No1 without a competitor in the American auto industry; the rich and famous and the wanna-be-famous all owned a Cadillac.

The most celebrated Cadillac was Al Capone's 1929 car which was actually used in the *Godfather* and The *Untouchables* movies, in fact every time a roaring twenties' gangster car was needed. The Capone Caddie also famously had two original bullet holes in the bodywork.

The North American Mustang P51 fighter plane was often called the "Cadillac" of the sky.

1953 CADILLAC FLEETWOOD SERIES 75

1957 Cadillac Eldorado Biarritz Convertible

With reference to lost Spanish gold, the Cadillac Eldorado encompasses a range of models from 1952 on. Early models have the signature big fins, again by Hollywood designer Harley Earl and co-designer Bill Mitchell, especially in the fifties.

One legendary yarn was that Earl and Mitchell argued over the size of the fins on the Eldorado. Mitchell raised them four inches and Earl didn't notice.

The 1957 Cadillac Seville was the hardtop and the Biarritz was the convertible with fairly simple fins and chipmunk cheek rear fenders. The trunk looks like you could fit a Fiat 500 Bambino in there.

Cadillac probably used the name Biarritz because it is a small seaside resort for the rich and famous in France just north of San Sebastian and the Spanish border, on the Bay of Biscay, with Seville being in Spain.

The '57 Biarritz proved to be a desirable Caddie in the classic car industry, with the name lasting until 1991.

You can imagine a '57 Caddie owner on his way to a first date wearing a *White Sport Coat and a Pink Carnation*...Marty Robbins released the pop song in 1957.

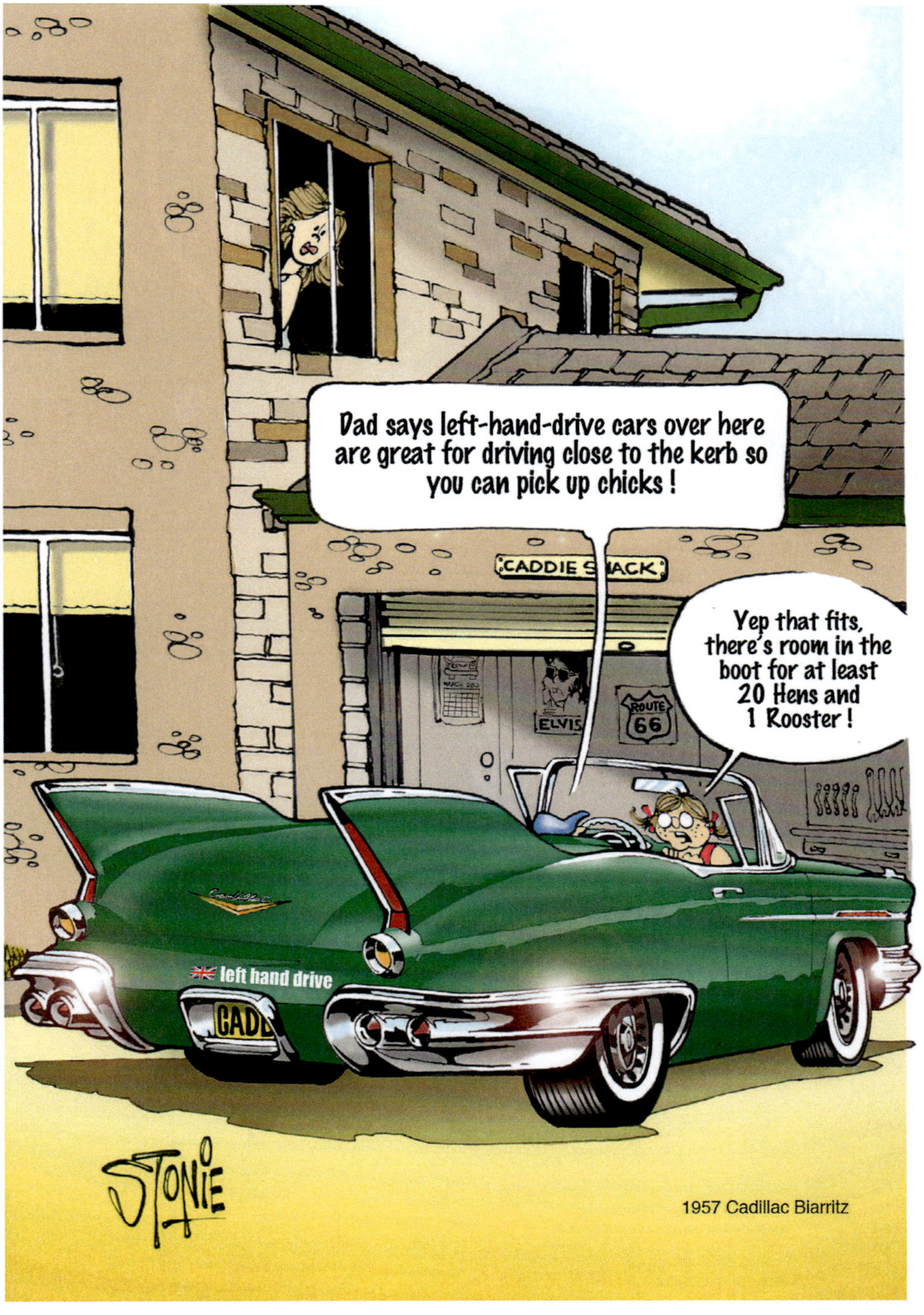

1957 Cadillac Biarritz

1936 Ford V8 Coupe

After the Second World War, teenage Americans old enough to drive started what we now know as the hot rod industry because they built, chopped and channelled cars from the thirties, fitting them with wide rims and no fenders. Even today the 1930s' Ford is one of the favourite models for hot-rodding.

Some retro restorers will, of course, stay with the flathead 221 cubic inch V8 which has a throb all of its own. It was often described as the "gangsters' car"; in fact in 1934 Clyde Barrow wrote a letter to Henry Ford congratulating him on a wonderful car. Bonnie and Clyde's Ford V8 was somewhat weighed down with lead bullets that put lots of holes in the body (and in them too).

The two-door 1936 Ford V8 Coupe, sometimes referred to as the Tudor, was a signature car used by the comic book detective Dick Tracy.

The Beach Boys' classic 1967 song the *Little Deuce Coupe* refers to this favourite Ford, "deuce" meaning "two" and "flathead mill" meaning an "engine" in surf talk. The lyrics also go..."I got the pink slip daddy", meaning the winner took the loser's car under street drag racing rules.

Old cars and surf music were 1960s' gold.

Hey Vinnie, so show me how you've restored my Ford coup...to look like a real Gangster's car !
WAKEFIELD
Castrol Regd.
MOTOR OIL
—the Product of an All-British Firm
FERODO
BRAKE LININGS
MEAN SAFETY
STONIE

1965 Oldsmobile Toronado FWD

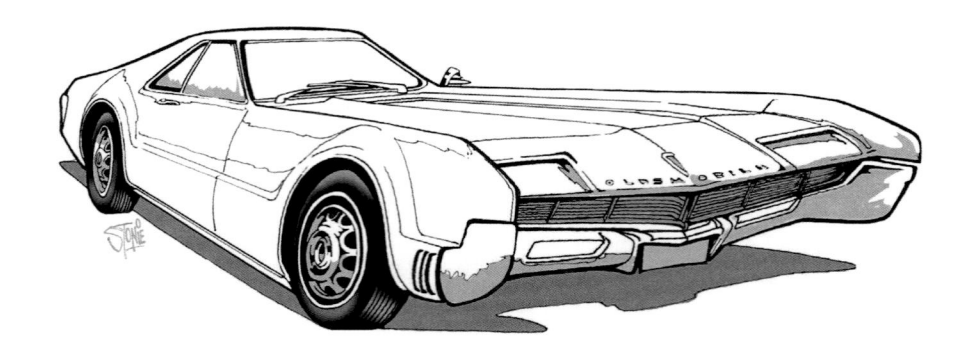

Rear-wheel drive versus front-wheel drive will always start a heated discussion in any bar, "You never put the cart in front of the Horse!" You might think the Americans would never entertain front-drive cars but the Cord 810 had a Lycomming seven-litre V8 with front-wheel drive before the Japanese attacked Pearl Harbor.

Two decades after the war, Oldsmobile (GM) asked designer David North to draft an image of a front-drive compact sports car but they did not really intend it for production. Oldsmobile changed their mind – when managers saw the artwork. However, an issue emerged with platform size, and, for cost reasons, GM went back to a bigger wheelbase.

While Ford had already patented a front-drive-designed model, Oldsmobile had been playing with a front-drive idea since 1958.

The massive engine bay of the yet-to-be-named Oldsmobile allowed a seven-litre – 425 engine to be married to a turbo-hydramatic three-speed auto to gear this "thing".

It was finally named Toronado, a made-up name for an earlier show car. However, as much as we all look at it today as a lumbering heap of twisted, tortured steel, the Toronado was third at the 1966 European Car of the Year awards, a feat no other American car has achieved before or since. Also the Toro won 1966 Car of the Year as voted by *MOTOR TREND (USA)*.

Current owners today love their Toronados and win lots of money hustling betting if it's front- or rear-wheel drive.

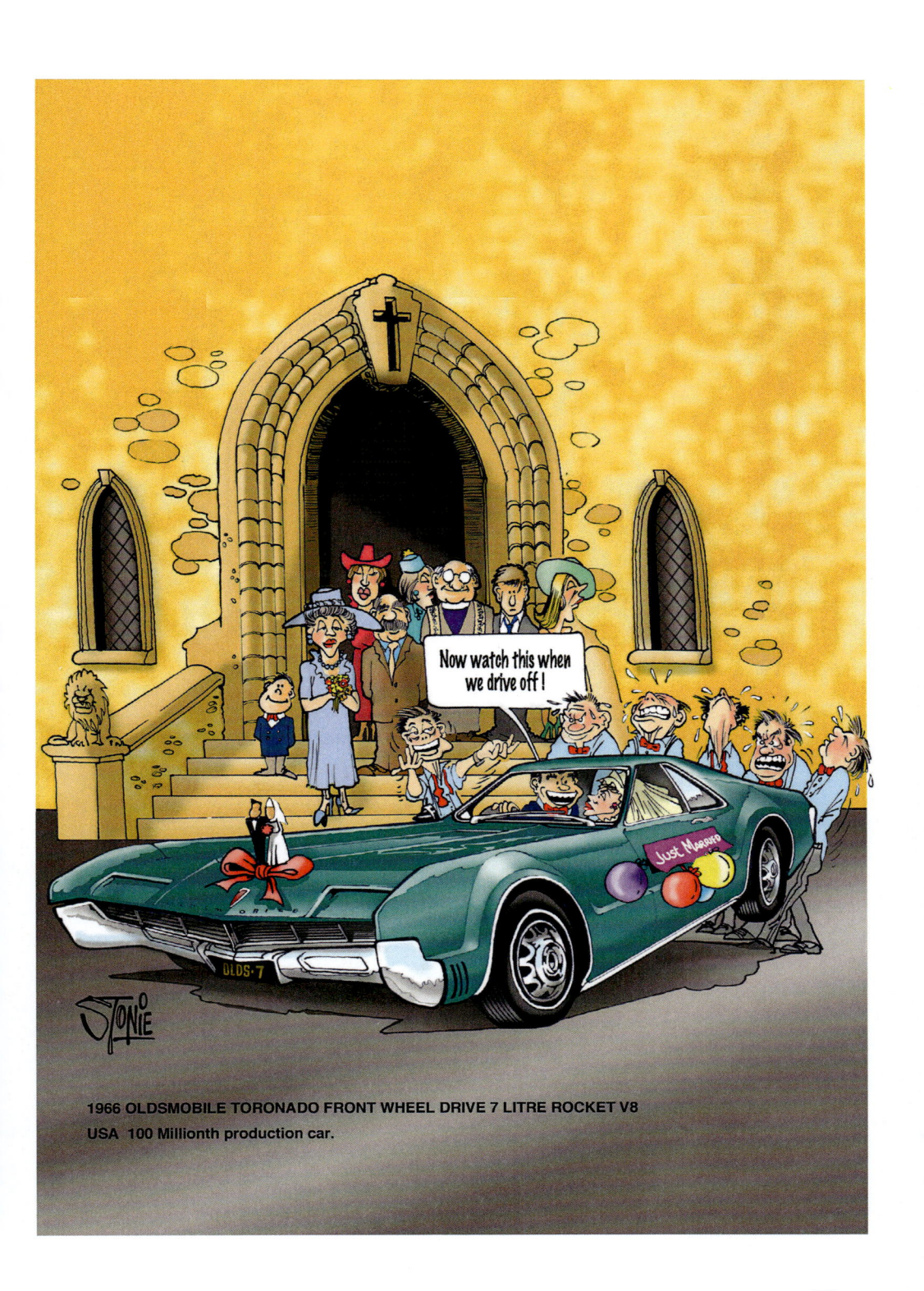

1966 OLDSMOBILE TORONADO FRONT WHEEL DRIVE 7 LITRE ROCKET V8
USA 100 Millionth production car.

1975 Porsche 930 Turbo

"It's like being kicked up the backside by an elephant!"

Most of the seventies' turbo cars had turbo lag like playing a pipe organ...You hit the keys and two seconds later you get a sound. The 1975 Porsche 911 Turbo was a bit like that and at the other end, take your foot off the gas and the bugger kept going with turbo run-on!

It seemed Porsche threw everything they had at this car to recover from a handling characteristic that the 911 supposedly had if you tried to drive it like a normal car. With big wide wheels, especially on the back, lots of suspension bits, big trumpet exhaust and a huge rear spoiler incorporating the intercooler core, the car was given the tag: "the whale tail Porsche".

Despite the German sports carmakers' effort to change from rear-engined cars to their new front-engined models, 924, 944 and the V8 928, their customers resisted, wanting to stay with the configuration of the 911. The classic flagship of the Porsche squadron is still that old 930 Turbo.

The urban myth is that when Porsche launched their new 1963 model called the 901 because it was the 901st project for the company, the French Peugeot people told Porsche, "No, you cannot use the zero!" and they still claim today they own the rights to any middle zero.

So the Germans called their next new production model the 911 and a legend was born. Today because "Nine-Eleven" has a catastrophic meaning, the most famous Porsche is now referred to as a "Nine-One-One"..."Hullo, Police!"

1975 Porsche 930 Turbo

1989 Nissan Figaro

You can't help but admire the diversity and humour of our Asian friends in the motor industry; they love the music of pomp and circumstance. Honda bring out a model called the Jazz so the Koreans at Hyundai call their market competitor Getz, after Stan Getz the jazz musician.

Somewhere deep in the bowels of Nissan Motor Corporation someone wanted to have fun and go retro, so Naoki Sakai and Shiji Takahashi were asked to design a mini luxury car along the lines of a Fiat Bambino 500, 2CV Citroën or the Mini Cooper.

Japan's congested main roads and tiny suburban lanes favour small vehicles, plus the homeland market loves the latest trend. The result was the Figaro, so named after the Mozart opera, the *Marriage of Figaro*.

The Figaro is no toy; it has air conditioning, leather seats, a CD player and a fixed top cab with sliding fabric roof, and is pulled by a 987cc turbo attached to a three-speed auto... perfect for the trending new-age hipster set.

Oh, and it comes in *four-seasons* of colours in a tribute to Vivaldi: Topaz Mist (autumn), Emerald Green (spring), Pale Aqua (summer) and Lapis Grey (winter). The original 8,000 production run had a second go of 12,000 on demand.

Nissan also brought out a small courier van and called it "S-Cargo" and snailed it! Don't laugh, it sold like hot scones.

1969 NISSAN FIGARO TURBO 1000cc FK10

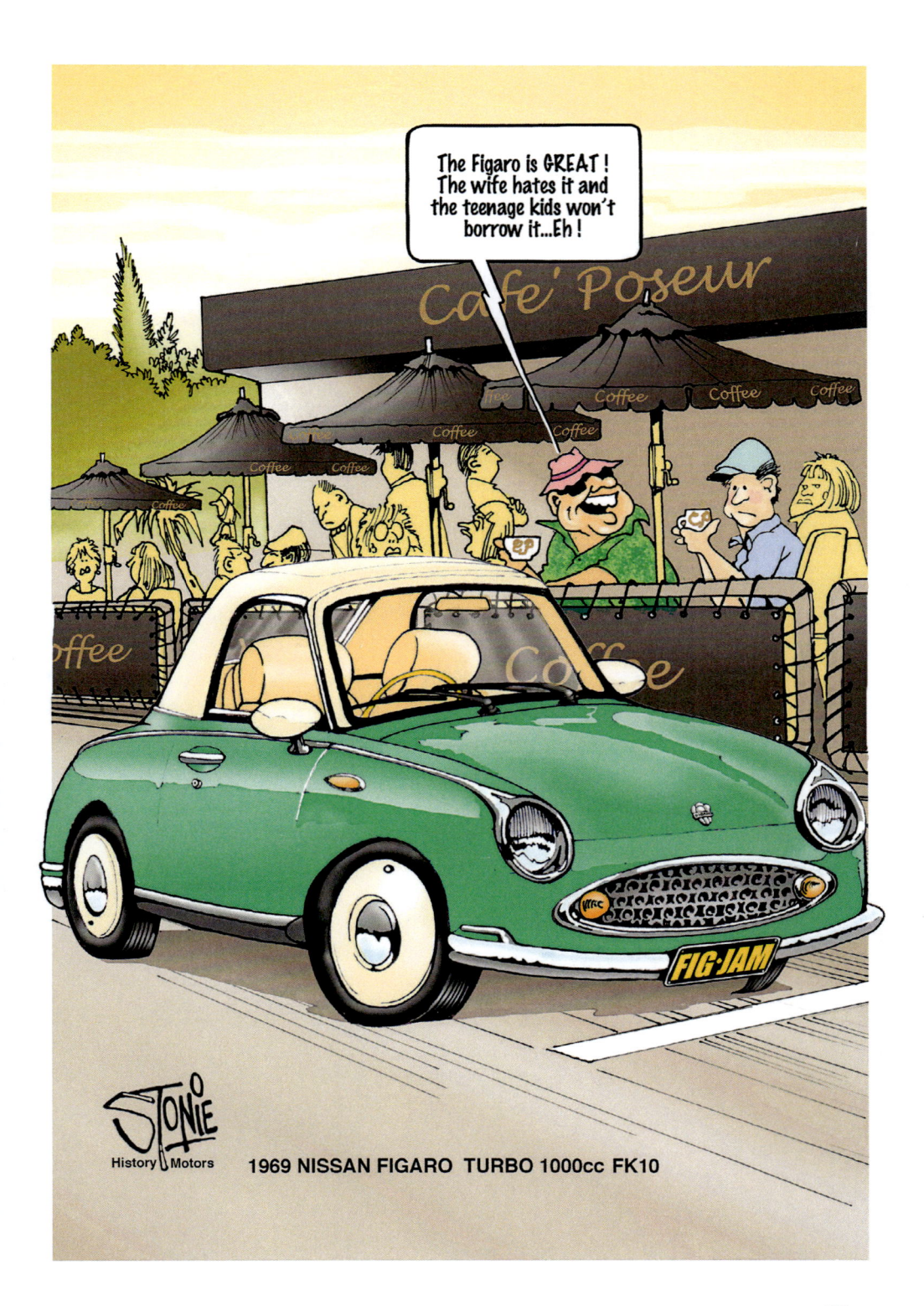

1957 Chevrolet Belair

Cuba's Havana City has a rolling automotive museum around its streets with hundreds of classic old American cars in good, bad and ugly condition. After the Cuban revolution in 1959, Fidel Castro put a total ban on American imports and since then the Cubans have maintained their classic American cars, remaking innovative spare parts to keep them running.

When President Obama announced there would be a concerted effort to renegociate a trade agreement with the republic, Cubans were allowed to buy new cars at exorbitant prices under the rule of Fidel's brother, Raul.

With Cuba just 90 miles from the Florida coast, American tourists can now visit and tour in any of the Cuban classic clunkers.

Hopefully the canny Cubans will realise their old cars could become a handy retirement fund and grapple with the gringo classic car collectors. It will be sad if the old clunkers completely disappear from the streets of Havana.

1957 Chevrolet Bel-Air 283ci V8

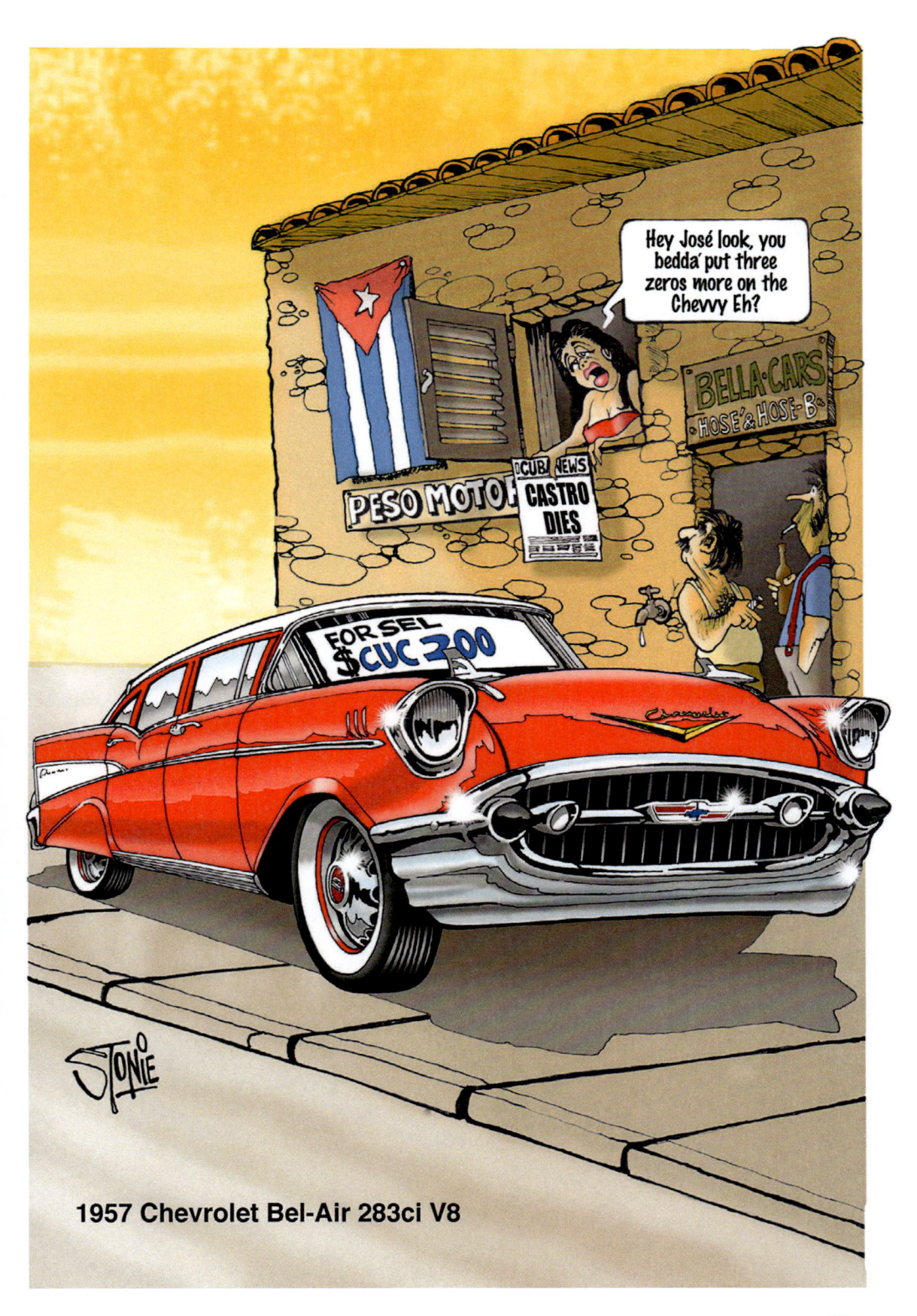

1934 Voisin C15 Saloit Roadster

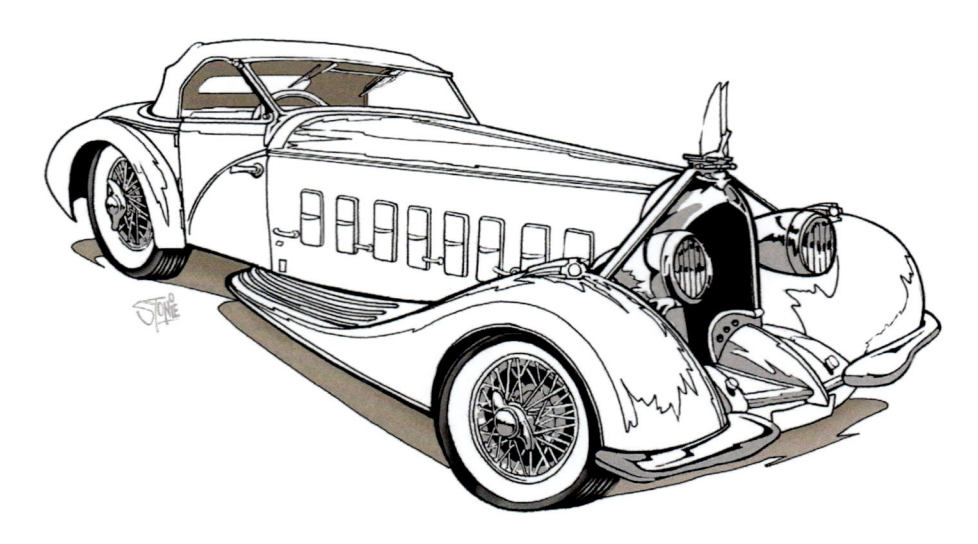

"Holy Moly, it is like a Bugatti Royale!"

Monsieur Gabriel Voisin was an aviation manufacturer who diverted his attention to making unique cars in 1919. The 1934 Voisin C15 Saloit roadster seems to be a one and only specially built car which years later in new hands won Best at Show at America's prestigious 2002 Pebble Beach Concours d'Elégance.

The then-owner, S.Mann, had gracefully restored the C15 after he acquired it in 1998. Even though the source of this chassis and its provenance of construction are a mystery, it is understandable that the judges at Pebble Beach were blinded by this car's beautiful body.

Go back to the thirties and Monsieur Delacluse commissioned the vehicle to be made from a Voisin base with a signature Saloit body denoting the suburb where it was built. There is no record of who designed it. Monsieur Delacluse wanted his own body style with an incredibly long engine bonnet; maybe it was his design.

The chassis was chopped and extended to accommodate the engine compartment. You would be forgiven for thinking that this beautiful car must come with a straight-twelve cylinder or even a V12, but no, the Voisin engine supplier at that time included a 2.5-litre Knight (sleevevalve) motor with twin Zenith carbies. This is a stunning one-off limo from a bygone era.

1934 VOISIN C15 SALOIT ROADSTER Merlin V12

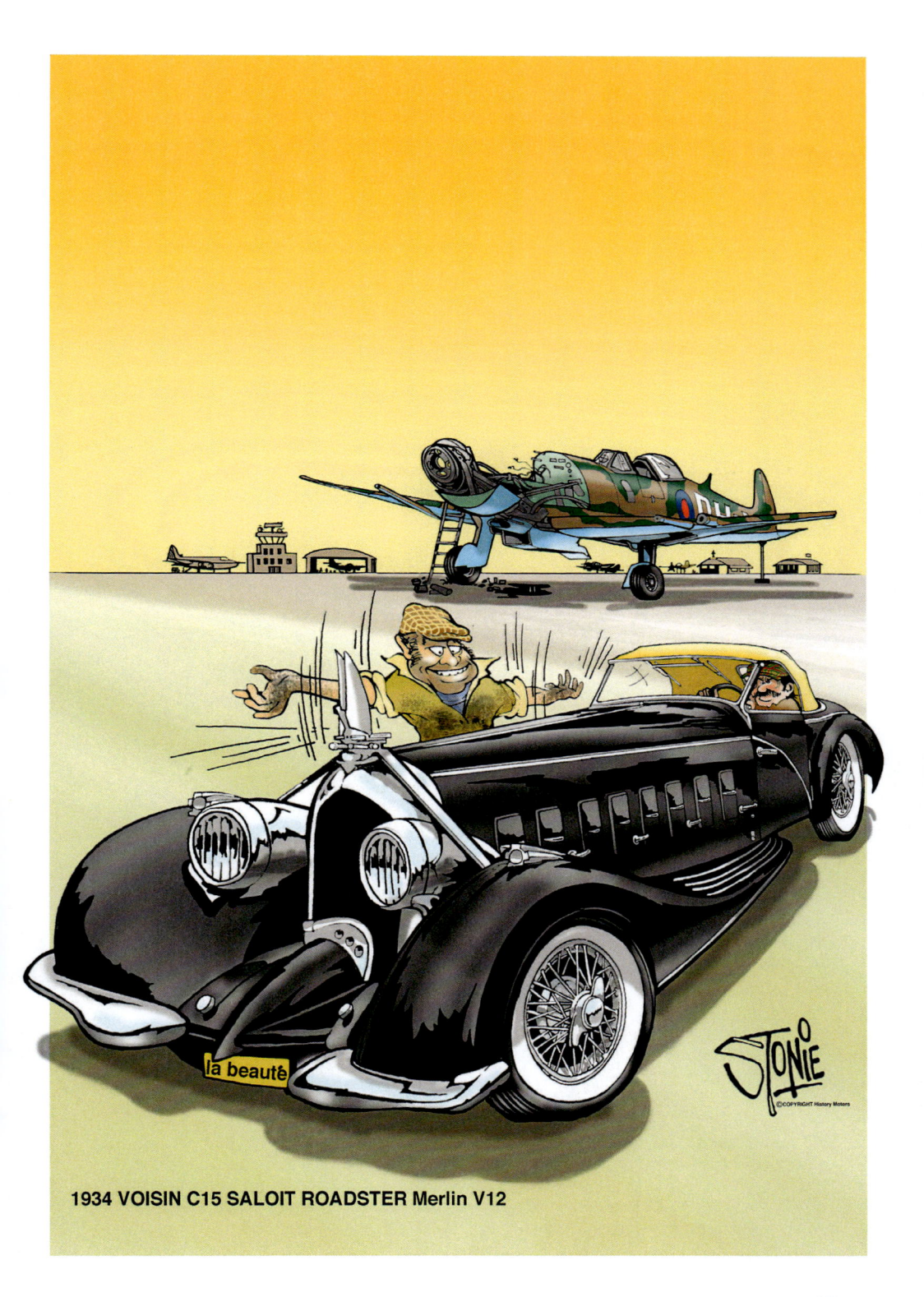

Father of the Mustang - Lee Iacocca

Plenty of stories have been written about the launch of the Ford Mustang in April 1964 from eager buyers camping outside dealerships to people parking a truck across a showroom driveway so they got the first choice of the new sports model sensation.

Henry Ford II charged his vice president, Lee Iacocca, with a project to come up with a new model to beat the General Motors Corvette, Camaro and Corvair Monza. The first clay model was a two-seater but Iacocca insisted that Americans like a rear seat, so the model-makers stretched it.

One of the many stories told was that, right up until the car was about to go into production, they still didn't know what to call the new sports Ford. Cougar was a consideration so a grille badge was made with an abstract cat in a rectangle. One of the designers replaced it with an emblem of a horse galloping from right to left. Iacocca saw it and remarked, "That race horse is going the wrong way." The designer replied, "It's not a race horse, it's a Mustang!"

There were other claims that Iaccoca named it after his gridIron team, the Mustangs, but the first story of the race horse is the one that stuck. In Germany Ford could not use the name and badged it possibly with a T18.

Opening scenes in the 1966 French classic movie *A Man and a Woman* of a red Mustang convertible doing donuts on a beach would have sold a few in Europe.

The Ford Mustang lives on today with a very good retro version of the fastback body with even a special Steve McQueen dark green *Bullitt* limited edition model.

50th Anniversary 1964 Ford Mustang 289 V8

1953 General Motors-Holden FJ

Holden & Frost in Adelaide, South Australia, were harness and leather manufacturers who had government contracts supplying the army with saddlery and drays for the cavalry during the 1899 Boer War. After the turn of the new century, Holdens naturally embraced the new motor car assembly business that later became a motor body builder between the world wars with draft plans from General Motors USA.

During the Second World War Holden Motor Body works built trucks and field guns for General Motors. After the war, with support from Prime Minister Ben Chifley, Holden engineers were sent to Detroit to develop an Australian-built car from the ground up. Simultaneously, General Motors had shelved an idea for a more compact saloon which was perfect for the Australian market and became the base for Holden's new car.

In 1948 Chifley stood at the end of the production line of the first Australian built General Motors-Holden car, affectionately called the "old roundie", officially named Model 48-215; it was unofficially deemed the "FX".

As often the case with model upgrades, it was the second Holden, the 53' FJ Holden, that became the star of the Australian car show. Whole families lived and breathed the Holden FJ. In fact, many people born in the fifties claim to have been conceived on the back seat of an FJ. Children were even named after the car, simply called "FJ".

The centrepiece of the FJ has to be the grinning mouth chrome grille. In modern times, so many FJs have been built out of spare parts or are upgraded 48-215s, it's said that there are more on the roads now than were ever made.

After nearly sixty years of motor car manufacturing and a successful motorsport tradition, General Motors-Holden built its last car on Friday 20th October 2017.

1953 FJ HOLDEN SPECIAL

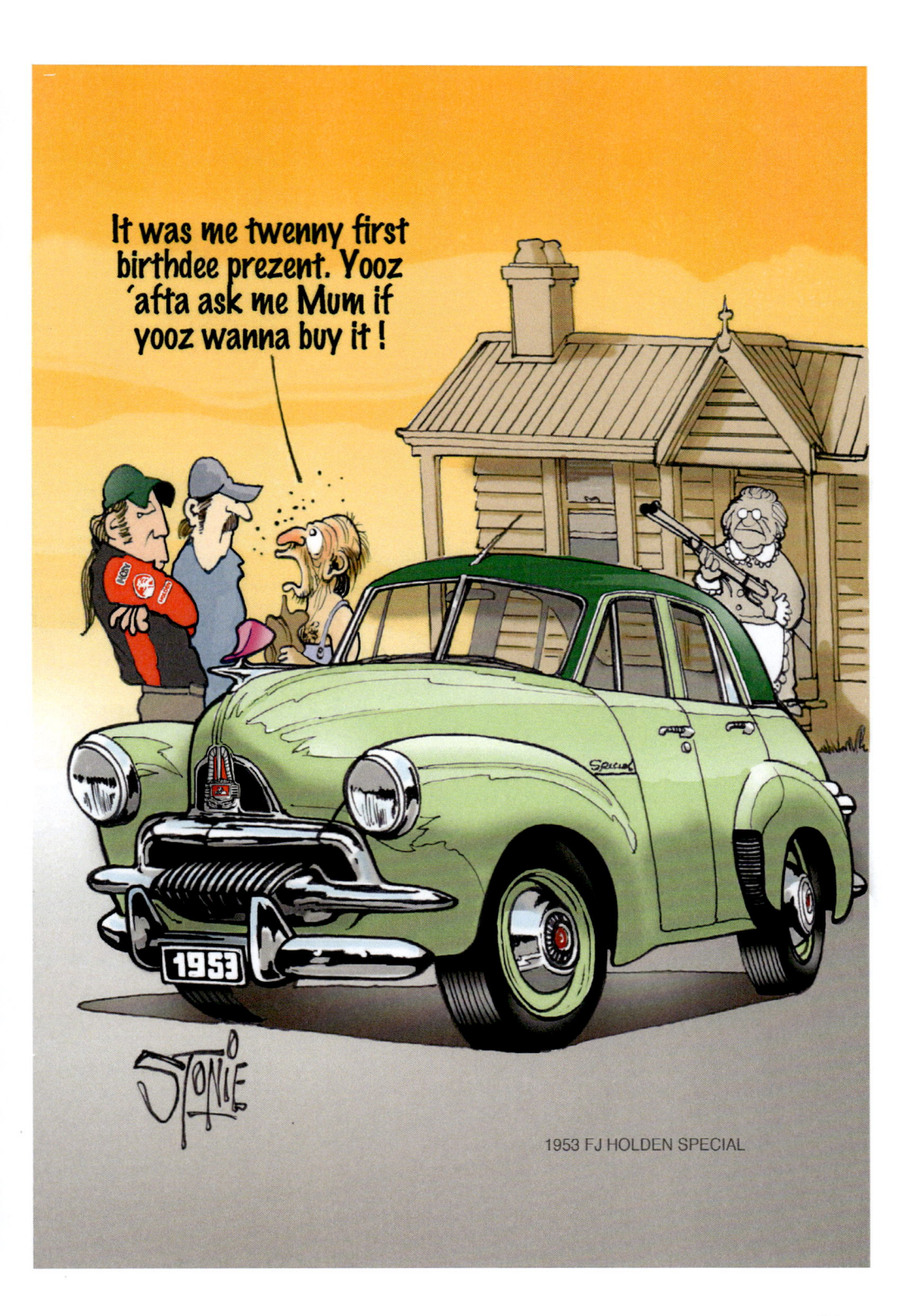

1955 Volkswagen Karmann Ghia

Modern day trends include anything that is uniquely different and uncomplicated. There were some great young car designers in post-war Europe that were given the opportunity to create something that was not only trendy in the sixties but became a stunning classic in this new century. The VW Karmann Ghia is more popular today than it ever was in 1955.

The Karmann Ghia has a simple aerodynamically shaped body styled by a young Italian fellow at Carrozzeria Ghia called Luigi Segre, who played with a flat-four 1100cc Volkswagen engine in a widened, almost hand-built body.

The German company Karmann were thrilled with the design, but the new Ghia coupé would be in a higher price bracket than the average Volkswagen Beetle. The first Karmann Ghia sold 365,000 of the coupé and over 80,000 of the rare cabriolet.

The Type 34 model of the Karmann Ghia is generally favoured as the classic Karmann Ghia rather than the later 1965 1500/1600 shape with sales of only 43,000. However, some will argue the later model with reshaped contoured headlights and the extra grunt is worth more because of the low production run.

American designer Walter D. Teague thought the Karmann Ghia was worthy of a place on his list of beautifully designed products.

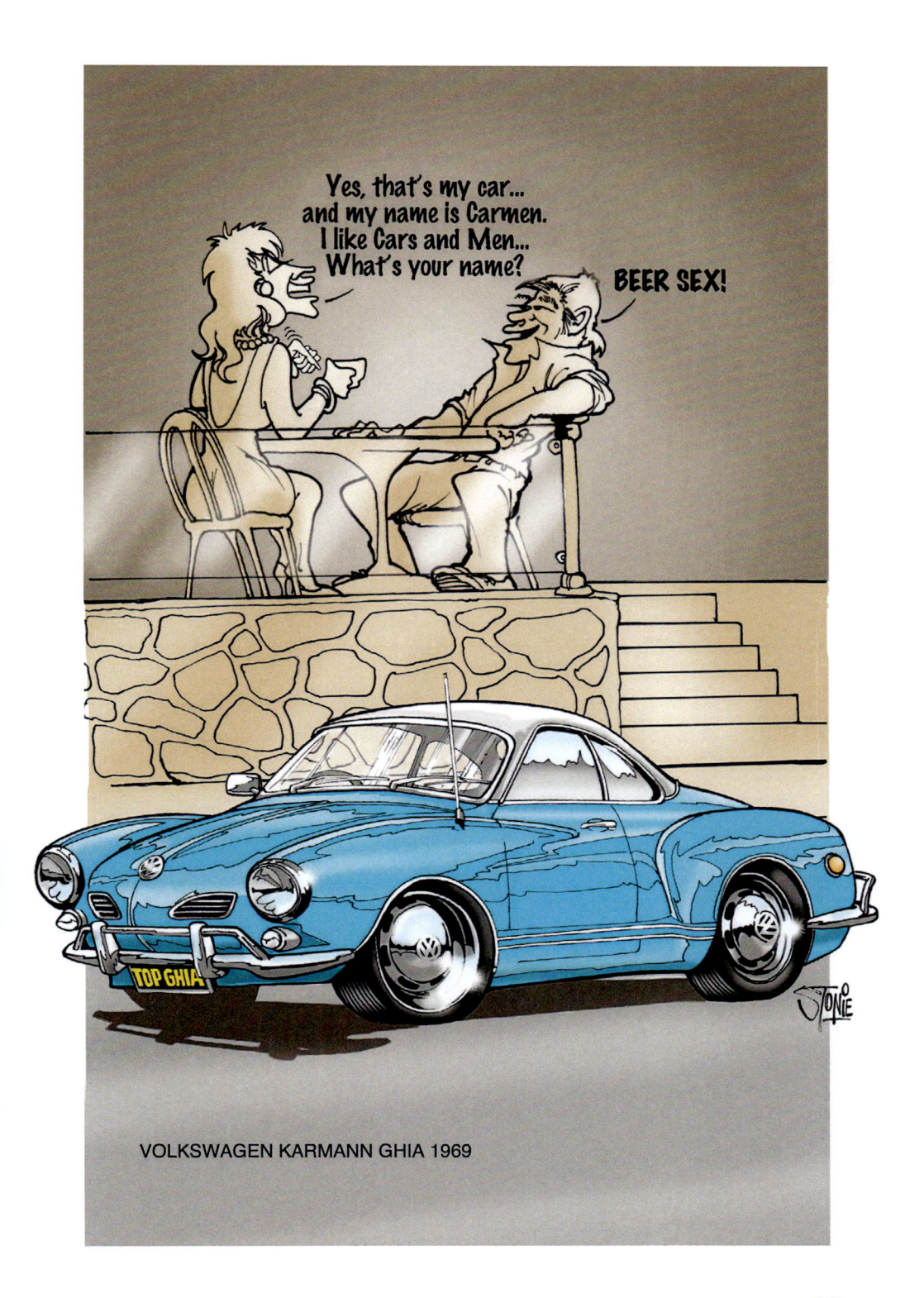

VOLKSWAGEN KARMANN GHIA 1969

1960 Goggomobile DART

The Daimler SP250 V8 fibreglass-bodied sports car was prevented from using the name Dart because of the famous American Dodge Dart which was a registered name around the world.

Microcars were a cheap necessity in a financially constrained Europe in the post-war fifties and the German Goggomobil car by Hans Glas was a good example of a cheap to run two-cylinder, two-stroke, air-cooled rear-engined runabout that would tootle around at 53mph and be a lot more weatherproof than a motorbike.

Australian motor fabricator Bill Buckle, saw an opportunity to sell Goggos in Oz and travelled ironically to Dingolfing in Bavaria to import the base cars to Australia. Bill had another idea, that it might be fun to build a sports body on the Goggo platform so tiny it wouldn't need doors.

The Goggomobil Dart was so cute it would fit in a building's service lift and, with a bigger 300cc engine, it would do 100km/h. It is possible that Billy patented the Dart as a "toy car" and that is why Chrysler didn't send the lawyers in after him.

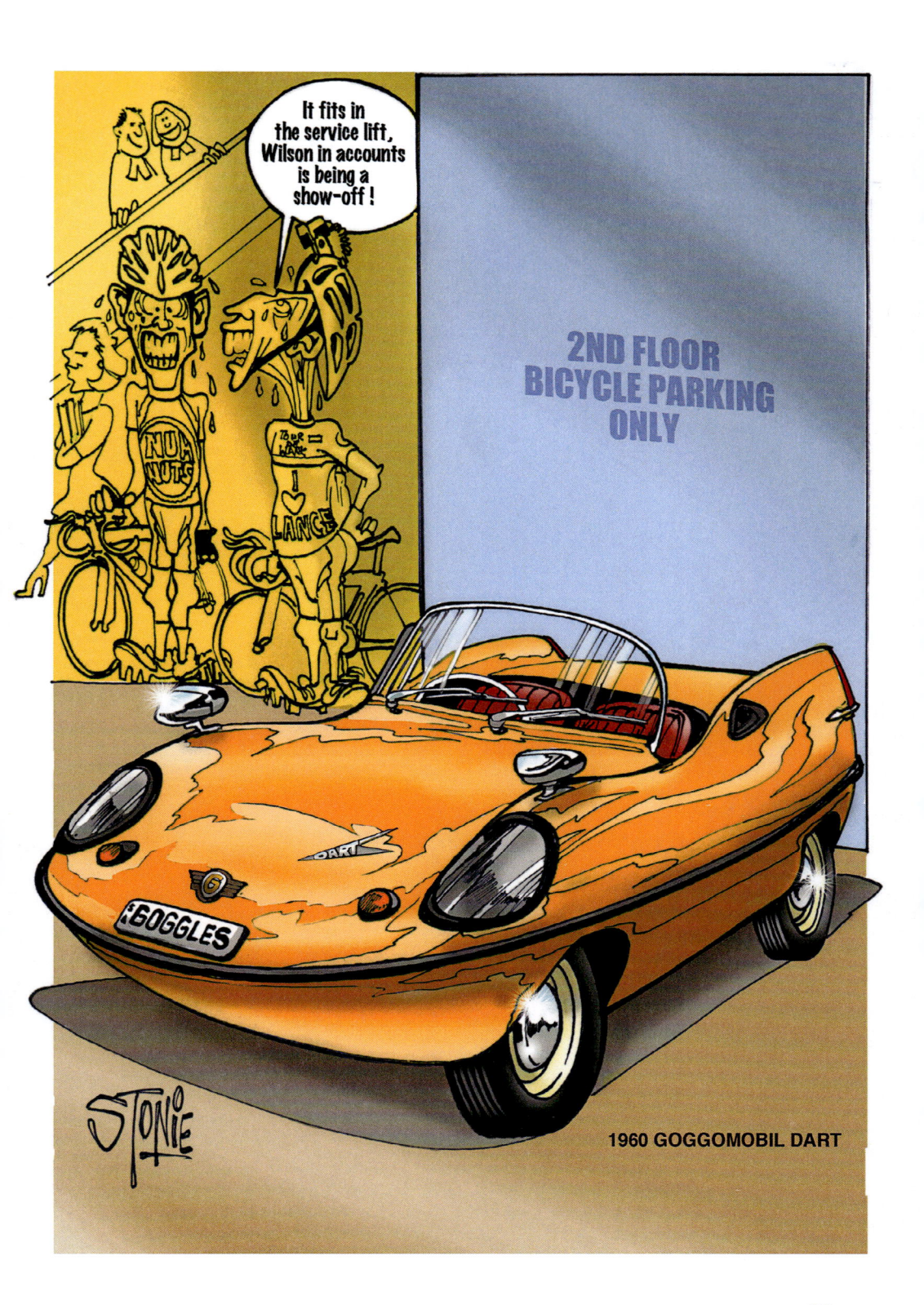

1960 GOGGOMOBIL DART

1966 Bedford TJ Series

Classic truck collectors are an interesting group and "truck ugly" is a real virus with some motoring collectors for whom, as kids, their first passion was a truck.

If you were born after WWII you would not get on a bus if it wasn't a Bedford and their trucks were everywhere as toys as well. Bedford was a British Vauxhall product and one truck model has gone through a rebirth in today's new classic era with private tradesmen restoring the TJ series.

Truck collectors seem not as precious about engine equipment originality. An engine change from the standard petrol or diesel to a lazy V8 does not result in a restorer's suicide. An original cabin interior is more important.

The grille back-panel and the heavy duty wheels chrome up a treat. Add a modern gloss paint job and a company logo on the doors and you have a rebirthed Bedford TJ tray top with character, almost too good to put a tool box in the back.

They were never that well finished!

BEDFORD J SERIES 1966

1959 Holden FC Special

By the time the sixties arrived, General Motors-Holden Australia had 50% share of the down under market over Ford Australia and BMC Australia who were both rebuilding knock-offs from overseas.

By the time the 1959 FC Holden hit the road, some families were deeply rooted in the culture of Holden being the all-Australian car. Ford and BMC Australia had to do something about it if they wanted to stay in the very small Australian market.

Ford designed and built the Aussie version of their US Falcon and later, BMC produced the monster P76 V8, bragging that you could fit a 44-gallon oil drum in the boot.

A Holden advertising agency jingle would set the carmaker in cement as a true blue Aussie manufacturer with the tag line... "Football, meat pies, kangaroos and Holden cars..." but, ah, no mention of beer.

HOLDEN FC SPECIAL 1959

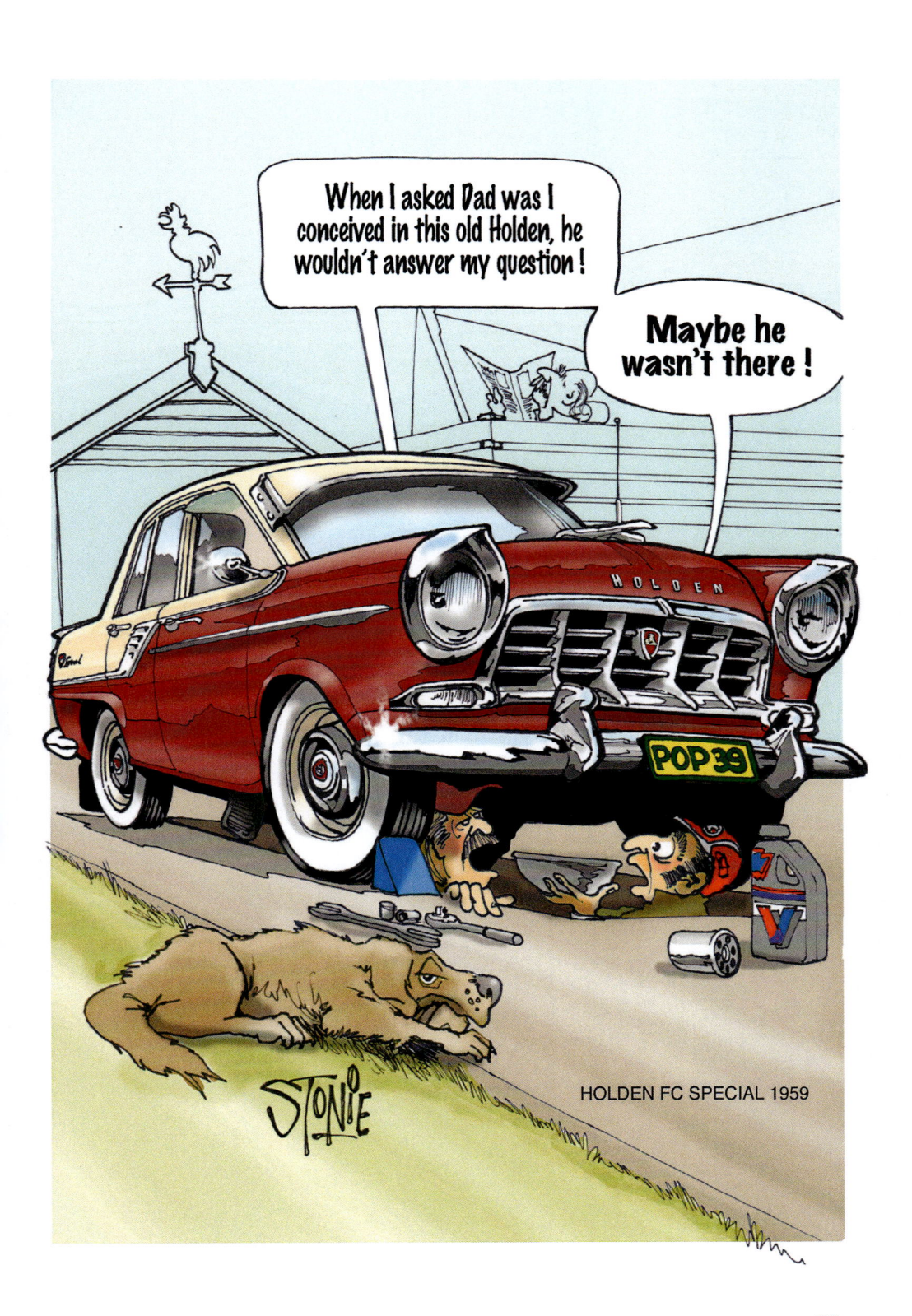

1935 Ford V8 Deluxe Roadster

Did the Americans invent the convertible or was it a flow-on from the fold-down horse-drawn buggy days and the first ragtop roadsters? The original difference between a cabriolet and a convertible was that a cabriolet is a roof that folds down leaving the side windows up and a convertible has removable side windows called, in the old days, "side curtains"!

Today it's all become a bit blurred and the best example might be the MGA which has a fold-down top with detachable side windows and the MGB which has a fold-down top with wind-up windows. A drophead coupe and cabrio can refer to a cabriolet.

Car racing from its early 1900s' beginnings deemed roadsters should be raced as they were built with their tops up for safety. Even removable hard tops soon proved they were better left on, as the cars were aerodynamically faster.

So cabriolets and convertibles were relegated to being poseur cars for wind-in-the-hair boulevard cruising car lovers.

Between the wars Ford were the kings of convertibles. In the mid-thirties, the prettiest was the 1935 two-door V8 Deluxe Roadster, affordable for the average middle-class driver. Hollywood stars like Gary Cooper were driving 1930 Derham Duesenberg convertibles!

This was also the era of the rumble seat, a fold-down rear seat out in the elements, instead of a luggage compartment. This rear seat was also known as a dickie seat!

Late in their career, the famous comedy team Laurel and Hardy used a 1935 Ford V8 Deluxe Roadster on film.

That 80-year-old car is just like me... Something seizes up, something starts to leak and something falls off !
STONIE

1965 Pontiac Bonneville Convertible

The first Pontiac Bonneville appeared at the General Motors Motorama car show in 1954 along with the new Chev Corvette. The Bonneville was a "long'n"... the station wagon topped 19 feet! The pride of the fleet, as always with Americans, was the convertible, a little lighter than the tin tops at 2.5 short tons!

A 370 255hp V8 with a four-barrel carby was still needed to haul this monster. The Ponty Bonneville was a big favourite for pace cars at the Indianapolis 500 and also a favourite drag car later.

Bonneville of course is the name of the famous salt flats in Utah which many motor manufacturers used as a test bed for new models. Early attempts at world auto land speed records for production cars were staged there.

Named after Benjamin Bonneville, a US Army man, the salt lake strip is twenty miles long, five miles to get up to speed, five miles to set your speed record and five miles to slow down. To have the time officially recorded, you have to make two runs. Sadly, reports today say the salt lake is slowly disappearing.

One of the best movies to celebrate the weird culture of salt racing was *The World's Fastest Indian* staring Anthony Hopkins, a true story of New Zealand engineer/racer Burt Munro. "Tony" Hopkins once told a yarn of his love of jumping in a car and just driving to relax and unwind especially when he resided in the USA. He reiterated sometimes, when in America he would find himself miles from nowhere, it was always the adventure he loved with the bonus that nobody knew who he was out there.

One trip he found himself on the other side of the Rocky Mountains where it was as flat as a salt lake and he drove into one solitary gas station back a ways from the tarmac. As he walked in the door in search of a coffee, a very large African American lady greeted him, "Goddamit I am havin' a baaaad day!" she exclaimed. "I ain't had a customer all day and who should be the only dude to walk into my diner...Hannibal Lecter!"

Lincoln never drove a Lincoln, a Shelby Cobra ain't a snake. Chevrolet ain't no French car, Studebaker ain't a young cook. A Dodge Barracuda ain't a fish, and a Pontiac Bonneville don't belong on these salt flats !
OGDEN
PROVO
SALT LAKE CITY
WENDOVER UTAH
BONNEVILLE
NEXT SPEED TRIALS AUG 29 SEPT 3 2015
RUN Watchya Brung
TURBO CARS: 5,102 feet above SEA LEVEL!
NO ENTRY
BONNEVILLE
STONIE
1965 PONTIAC BONNEVILLE CONVERTIBLE 421cui

1969 Holden Monaro GTS 350 Coupé

Australian General Motors-Holden were originally the only production arm of the Detroit giant that ignored the US GM rule of "no motorsport". The clandestine factory racing team was formed under the banner of being a dealer team. Of course the local factory had to be involved, because the necessary engine and parts for racing had to be homologated.

Monaro, meaning "high place" in an Australian indigenous people's language, was the name given to the 1969 Monaro GTS. It had a European Opel style body with a big American V8 350 cubic inch motor. These models were also exported to South Africa badged as Chevrolets, a little poke in the eye for GM HQ in Detroit.

In 1969 the so-named Holden Dealer Team Monaro won the prestigious production car Bathurst 1000 motor race. Sales of Holden cars after the Bathurst win proved the value of racing the product, giving the model a value-added image.

In the seventies you could pick up a Monaro for $2000 but 20 years later suddenly Aussie muscle cars became the latest classic six-figure investment. Today any Holden Monaro is worth the price of a small farm.

The Australian Ford versus Holden V8 Supercar racing series became the NASCAR of the Australian and New Zealand motor sport calendar.

Ralf ! get your bum out here now! This old fart wants to buy that old Holden in the creek for "TWO BLOODY GRAND" !
HOLDEN
GTS
MANGO
STONIE

1955 Mercedes-Benz 300 SL Coupé

The fifties were the start of the "real" sports car era in the eyes of many car collectors. Certainly the carmakers were connecting their sports models with the new Formula One World Championship cars...none more so than Mercedes-Benz.

The W196 Grand Prix car was the fashionista image to aspire to, for the inner driver, with the introduction at the 1954 New York motor show of the Mercedes-Benz 300 SL Gullwing. This was the street version of the Stirling Moss/Denis Jenkinson Mille-Migia-winning sportscar and the coupé in the Pan American road race.

On sale in 1955, "SL" is not for "Super Luxury" but for "Sport Leicht" (sports light). Firsts for the stunning 300SL were direct fuel injection on a straight-six production car, a space-framed, all-alloy body and the first signature gullwing doors on a two-seater coupé. The fastest production car of its era...140mph!

Only Mercedes would have the patience to engineer gullwing doors that were structurally rigid enough without causing warranty problems. Every six-footer in the sports car market cheered, "At last a sports car we can get in and out of without wearing a back brace or needing a chiropractor!"

To please the shop window poseurs a 300SL convertible with a vertical headlamp cluster was launched in 1957. Very few mainstream manufacturers attempted the gullwing door system, except for some kit car plastic models and of course the bewildering De Lorean.

Whenever gullwing is mentioned, we all think of the Mercedes-Benz 300SL.

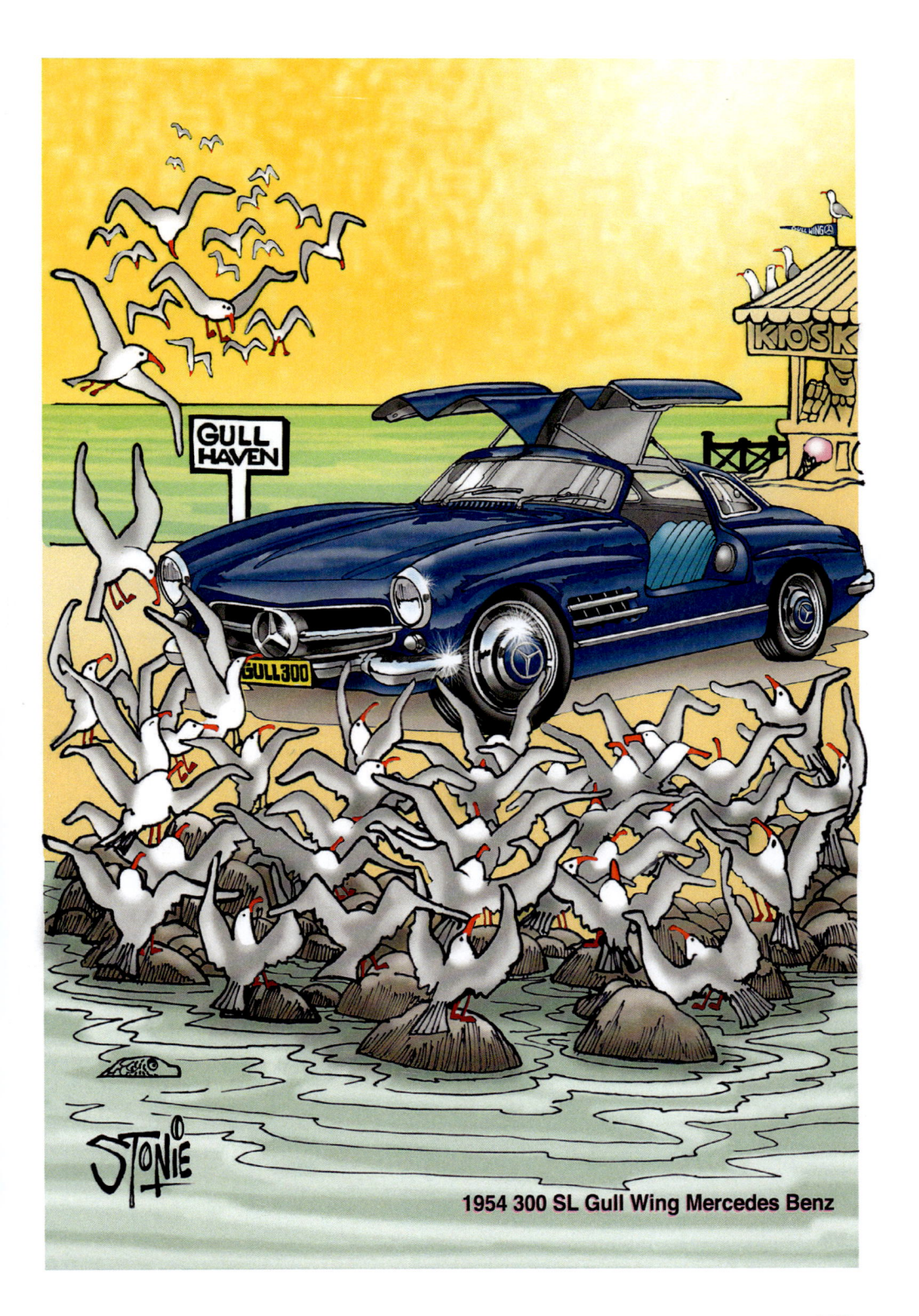

1954 300 SL Gull Wing Mercedes Benz

1958 Austin Healey MK1 Sprite

Would anyone buy a little sports car with no door handles, no wind-up windows, no trunk-luggage area and with headlights in the "up" position making it look like a frog, for £669? Well they certainly did in 1958, as it was the first model of the classic Austin Healey Sprite.

It was nicknamed the "Frogeye" from the day it was launched at the Monaco Grand Prix in 1958. It would seem the headlights were mounted where they are to comply with the US regulations at the time. Although pop-up headlamps were in the original design, budget constraints left them and a luggage compartment on the cutting room floor.

Open-top cars suffer a degree of scuttle shake which is a result of the flex in the body without the integral strength of a roof. Fortunately, with full chassis cars in the '50s and '60s, there was no measurement for scuttle shake until later with some monocoque open-top body styles.

The Donald Healey Motor Company's chassis designer, Barry Bilbie, linked the rear suspension posts of the Sprite Mark I to the body floor pan, described as a "unitary construction" with a complete nose-cone lift-up engine bonnet like a Jaguar racing car. This was a good step to making the monocoque body a little more rigid.

An A-series 948cc BMC engine with twin SU carbies and rorty exhaust burble could encourage an 80mph top speed with bumpy suspension to make hilly curves huge fun. Elsewhere in the world, it was often called the "bug eyed Sprite". Nearly 50,000 were made giving the Sprogg a healthy collectable price if you can find one for sale.

Owners formed their own breakaway clubs from the Austin Healey and MG groups and continued as stand-alone identities as the Sprite bounced from Mark II versions to a rebadged MG Midget model aptly nicknamed a Spridget.

You won't get a frog eyed Sprite for £669 anymore, try £8-10k for starters and don't turn your nose up at Sprites cocked and loaded with a 1275 Cooper S engine plus twin Webers.

1958 Austin Healey Mark 1 Sprite "Frogeye"

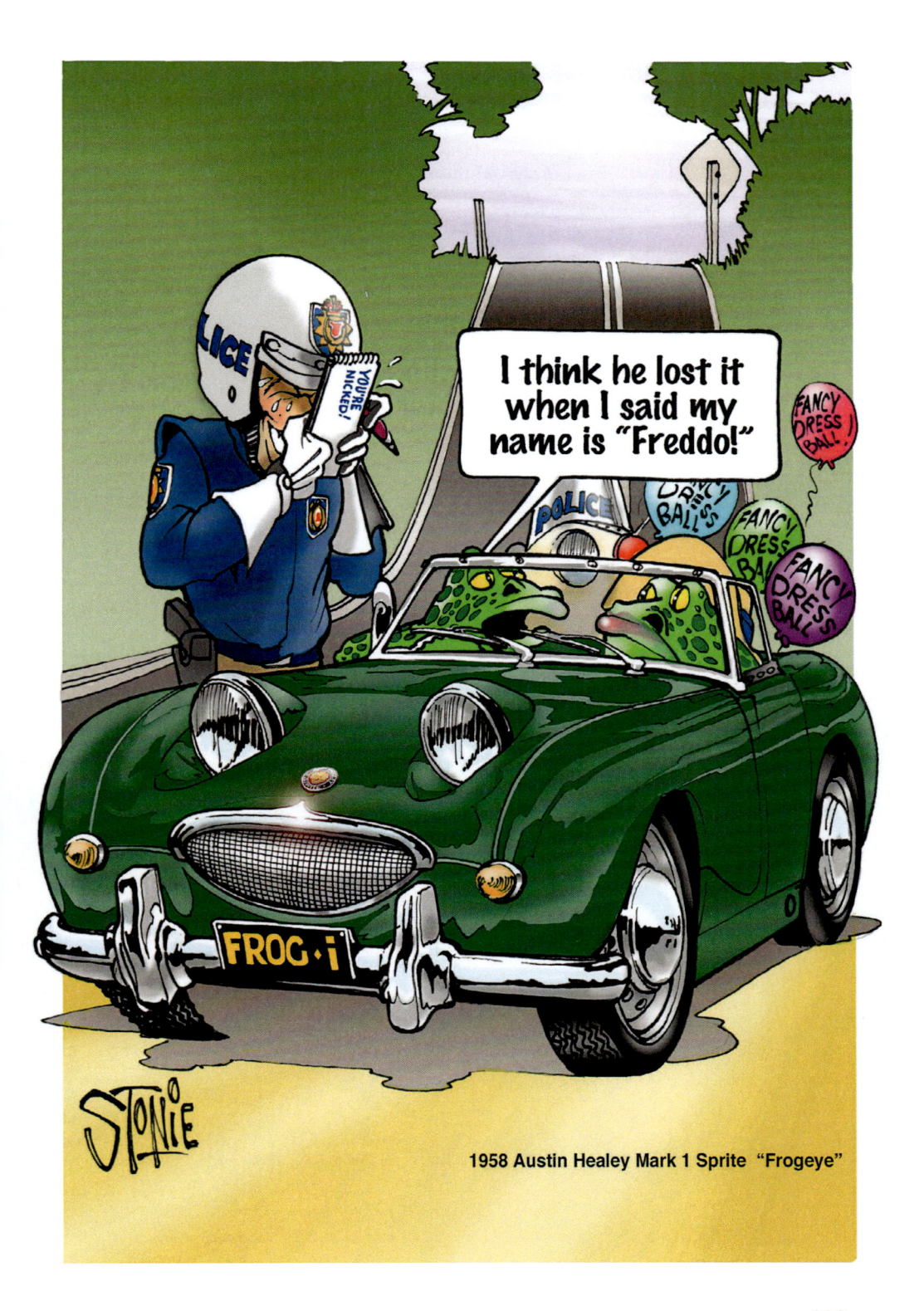

TV & FILM CARS

AFTER THE ITALIAN JOB
I think I get hit in the bloody head with a brick before I catch a fish in disa' river !
STONIE

STONIE
The boys are quiet tonight !
BHC
661

EVO X 'BABY'
17
SMAll FAMILY RA
STONIE

1933 Duesenberg SJ Speedster

Another movie with interesting automobile product placement is *The Great Gatsby*. The first version starred Alan Ladd in 1949, but the most remembered is the 1974 *Gatsby* with Robert Redford and Mia Farrow.

The 1974 Great *Gatsby* car chase scene with Robert Redford used a yellow Rolls-Royce Phantom which supposedly was what F. Scott Fitzgerald described in his book.

The Australian filmmaker Baz Luhrmann did an upbeat remake of *Gatsby*. Because the Alan Ladd version used **real** Duesenberg monsters, Baz bought two replica Duesenbergs so he wouldn't have had an insurance bill worth more than the film budget. These had fibreglass bodies and Ford V8 engines so could be quite rightly thrashed a bit more in his car-chase scenes.

The original Duesenberg SJ speedster boatbacks were only for the rich and famous. The huge seven-litre straight-eight with a blower (supercharger) was capable of a modest 120mph. The specs don't list any type of brakes but a parachute, like on a dragster, would have been helpful!

E.L. Cord of Auburn Automobile took over the Duesenberg Corporation in 1926. Auburn, of course, made the wonderful Cord and Auburn cars which were more predictable front-wheel drives than the Duezies. Maybe that's where the saying "It's a doozy" came from?

Hollywood actor Gary Cooper drove a Duesenberg roadster.

1933 Duesenberg SJ Speedster

1966-72 Lamborghini Miura

Movie actor Rossano Brazzi driving while smoking a cigarette in a Lamborghini Miura through the Italian Alps to the voice of Matt Monro singing *On Days like These* was the wonderful opening scene of the famous 1969 movie *The Italian Job*.

It was nothing short of orgasmic to any person who has driven a sports car on a mountain road, nearly as good as the images of the Ferrari speeding through early morning Paris in the famous underground film clip *Rendezvous*.

Product placement of motor vehicles in motion pictures is an art form if the company has the balls to accept the right offer for the best movie. The 1969 *Italian* Job is one of those classic movies that will glue you to the screen, then rip your stomach out when the Lamborghini Miura slams into a bulldozer bucket and is dumped over a cliff... I hope Lamborghini took the engine out before the body went over the edge.

Against the wishes of Ferruccio Lamborghini, engineers Dallara, Stanzani and the Kiwi Wallace planned the production of the Miura in their own time. Bertone designer Marcello Gandini created the body to grace the rear mid-engined east-west-mounted V12 with a shape ideal for the fastest production car in the world at that time.

Ferruccio Lamborghini was born under the sign of Taurus, was rumoured to be a bull fighting fan and the Lamborghini badge features a bull. The Miura was named after Lamborghini's friend, Eduardo Miura a famous Spanish fighting-bull breeder. They only made about 700, but the Miura is still the best-looking Lambo ever, if you have grey hair and own a bank.

1966 LAMBORGHINI MIURA SV

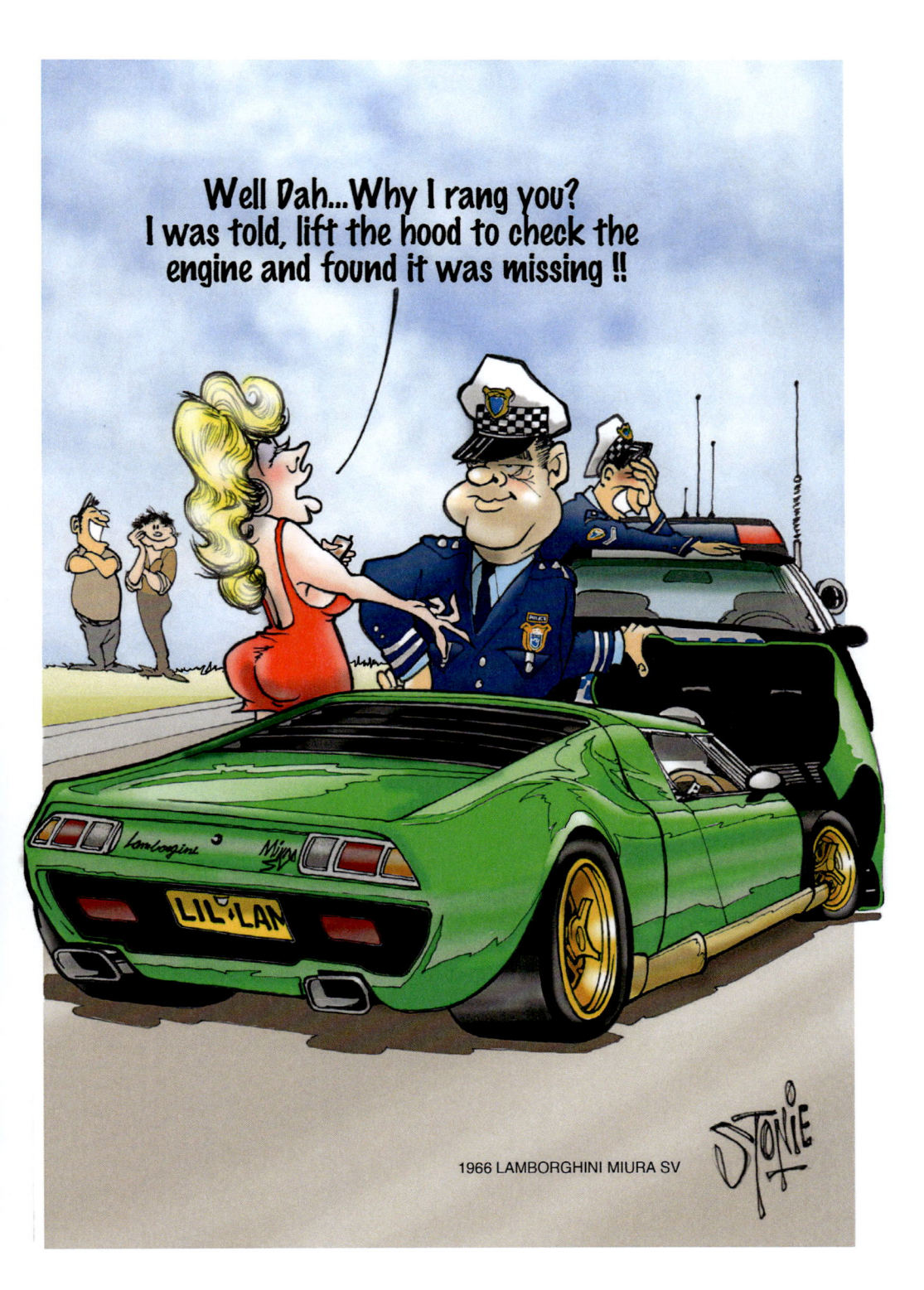

Corvettes, Stingrays and TV's Route 66

The famous Route 66 pop song was written by Bobby Troup who drove highway US40 and US66 (as they were originally signposted) in a 1941 Buick with wife Cynthia. Cyn' coined the line, "Get your kicks on Route 66!"

The song was first recorded by Nat King Cole in 1946, but much later was the Chuck Berry version, recorded again by the Rolling Stones in 1964, most remembered for the classic Berry guitar riffs!

The television series *Route 66* theme song was written and played by Nelson Riddle and his orchestra but is only remembered by a few post-war TV tragics.

The product placement in the Route 66 TV series of a Chevy Corvette was a brilliant choice, but over the years a lot of money has changed hands over which model was used. Was it a Stingray or the C1 twin headlight 1961-62 model? Well, it was first the C1 Corvette and later the 1963 "Shark" shape Stingray may have been used, so keep your money.

Martin Milner (Todd) and George Matharis (Buzz) travelled America en route to their adventures, inspiring baby boomers later to put the legendary drive on their bucket lists.

The animated movie *Cars* reinvented Route 66 as it was about rediscovering the famous highway. Lonely Planet has a good guide to follow the old route that is now a bit disjointed, showing only a few old gas stations and motel relics. However, there are a number of merchandise shops and a museum. Route 66 is still an icon of American history.

Despite the American pronunciation of "route" as "rowt", "Route 66" is pronounced "root 66".

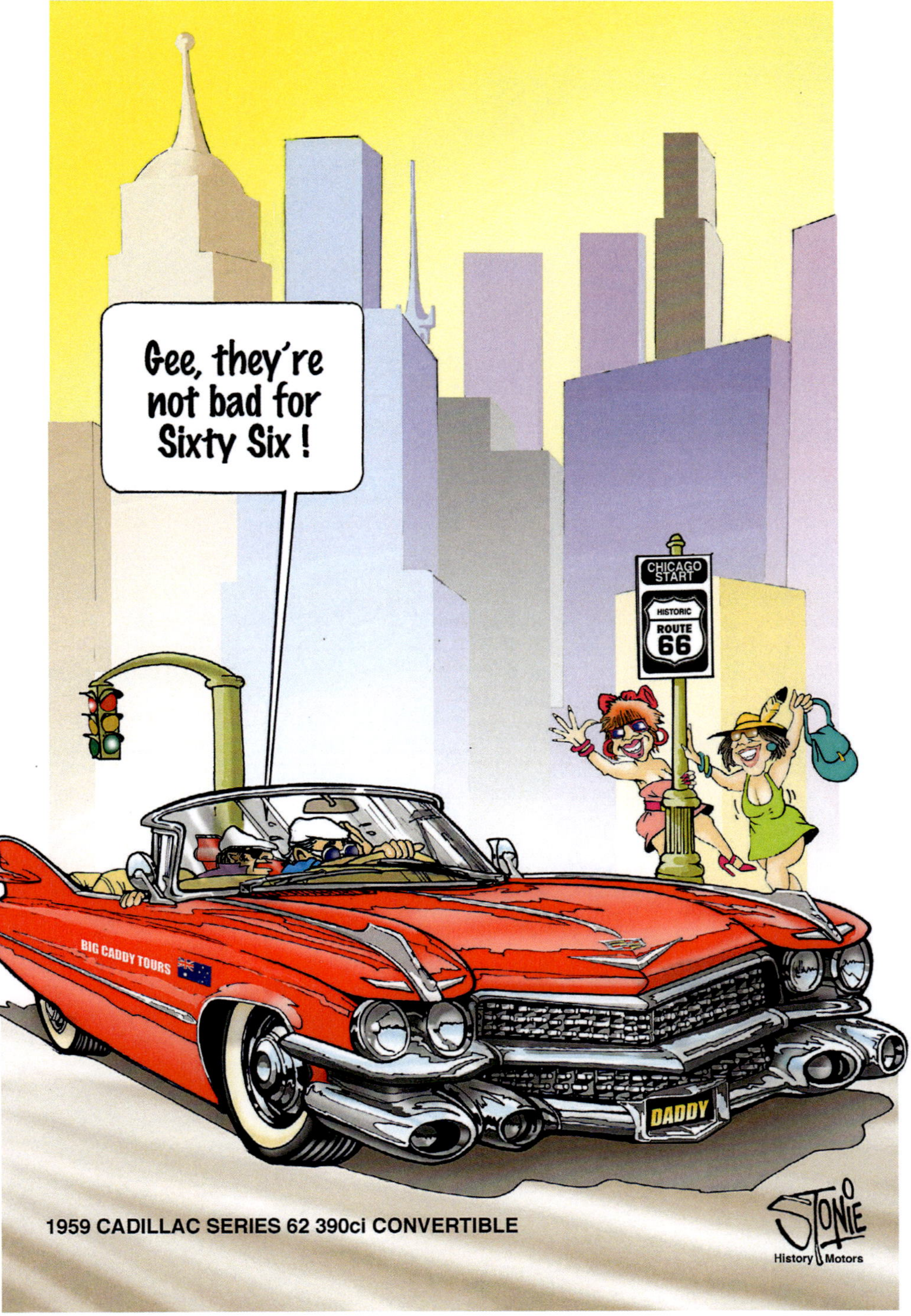

1959 CADILLAC SERIES 62 390ci CONVERTIBLE

1965 Aston Martin DB5

The most famous Aston Martin in the world is the James Bond DB5 in the 1964 movie *Goldfinger* plus in seven more 007 motion pictures after that. The four-litre 282bhp all-alloy engine with triple SU carbies would push air to 145mph.

Aston Martin management at first were opposed to supplying a car for *Goldfinger* but thankfully a deal for product placement was done as more than one car would be needed. The main DB5 it is thought was a prototype and an extra DB5 was needed for the action stunts. Two DB5s were modified and used as promotional cars at the movie's release locations and it is believed that much later one of these PR Cars fetched a lazy £1 million.

Most of the famous gadgets were not really on the car, like the knock-off twirling blades and the ejection seat. As the Aston travelled through each of the following James Bond movies more new gadgets appeared. Leapfrog to the Daniel Craig Bond movie classic *Skyfall*, and the original Aston DB5 reappeared only to be blown to bits in the final scenes. Hopefully, it was a model.

The 007 Aston Martin DB5 rates with the best of product placement film cars like the VW Beetle Herbie, Steve McQueen's fast-back Mustang in *Bullitt*, the Mini Coopers in The *Italian* Job, the Dodge Challenger in *Vanishing Point* and the girlfriend-killing Chrysler in the horror movie *Christine*.

In 2018 Aston Martin announced they would produce 28 authentic reproductions of the Goldfinger *film* car with some of the gadgets made famous in the movie. Twenty-five were offered for sale at almost £3 million each and sold out almost immediately! The replica 007 DB5s were finished in 2019 but are not permitted to be driven on public roads. The ejection seat will not feature in the list of trick-bits but I'll bet someone will try and fit an aftermarket accessory, even if not in working order.

The Goldfinger 1965 DB5 Aston Martin

1968 Fiat 500D

"Bambino" was really just a nickname for Fiat's 500D post-war city car, purposely designed microcar for the mad Italian traffic. Before the war the Topolino (little mouse) Fiat was a front-engined 500cc city car. However the 1957 Nuova (new) 500D had the engine (479cc) in the back as the new age Volkswagen Beetle had for the Germans and the Renault Dauphine had for the French.

Italian movies loved to feature tiny Bambinos on the big screen with long-legged women opening the "suicide doors".

Fiat also made a cute station wagon version called a Giardiniera Estate. The high performance works department, Abarth, engineered a sports race version which had a prop-up lever to open the engine cover and keep it cool when competing. The Fiat 500 Abarth was the Italian equivalent of a Mini Cooper.

The 1960 500 model increased the engine size to a proper 499cc and in the 1965 500F, they moved the door hinges to the front preventing the Italian ladies from showing too much underwear.

Future Fiat 500 models from 1968 to 1972 were deemed the Lusso (luxury) models and between 1972 and 1975 the 500R had a 594cc engine with an all-synchromesh gearbox but ah, to save money there was no fuel gauge, just a low-petrol light which gave you no warning at all...Well, I guess it was a purpose-built city car.

Following the success of the BMW Mini in the new millennium, Fiat rebirthed a modern-day Fiat Bambino, including an Abarth version, and they are now like belly-buttons... everyone has one!

FIAT 500D 1965

PETERBILT 281 PRIME MOVER 1960
FROM 1970 Movie "Duel"

1964 Volvo P1800S

After a rocky start in the late fifties, Volvo's planned sports version, which was to appeal to the important US market, could not find a suitable manufacturer. Volvo engineer, Helmer Petterson's son Pelle, was the designer commissioned to the drawing board as he worked for the Italian design team Pietro Frua, part of the Ghia group.

Helmer wanted Karmann to build the new Volvo but, halfway through the preparation, Volkswagen exexcutives said, "Nein das ist verboten!" Finally Volvo found the British company and Jensen would build its P1800. However, in 1963 Volvo moved the build back to home base, and thus began the P1800 "S" (for Sweden).

You could say the design was like a good whisky; it required a certain taste and although heavy and underpowered, it had a certain appeal in the market. Besides, it wasn't going to kill you.

The big break came for the sensuous Volvo when a TV company was knocked back on product placing the E-Type Jaguar in a new TV sleuth series. They approached Volvo who said yes.The TV series *The Saint* was a huge advertisement for the P1800S and Roger Moore, who played the lead as Simon Templar, was a car enthusiast. He threw on a set of Minilite racing wheels to match Volvo's rally image and the P1800S then became a star.

The late Roger Moore had a flair for film cars as he drove an Aston Martin DBS with Tony Curtis, who drove a Ferrari 246 Dino, as crime fighters in the TV show *The Persuaders*. In another auto promo Roger Moore, as James Bond, drowned a Lotus Esprit S1 in the movie *The Spy Who Loved Me*. There was also a Rover P5B V8 he crashed in the very forgettable 1970 film *The Man Who Haunted Himself*.

Volvo P1800S 1969

1973 Rover P5B Coupé V8

Prime Minister Margaret Thatcher was provided with a black Rover P5B V8 which was the ideal "Ministerial" conveyance. Also known as the "doctor's car", this Rover was no dog. The previous long running model P5 three-litre, six-cylinder full-chassis body was the base for the P5B.

The P5B coupé roof line was lower and the car was shod with Rostyle chrome wheels. The signature long-range driving lights moulded under the head lights either side of the wide-open-mouth grille gave this modest British vehicle a nice stance.

The 160bhp alloy V8 was not the Daimler 2.5 bored out. The "B" of the P5 denotes a remarkable Buick engine design which was to become one of the smoothest 3.5-litre power plants the British ever produced, cruising happily at 100mph. With that, the P5B had much-needed power steering and was only available in automatic.

The 3.5-litre V8 stayed with all Rovers including the P5B, the P6B, the SD1, the Land Rover and the early classic Range Rovers.

A P5B Rover with its standout instrument binnacle, leather and wood interior is an auto collectable for those with a modest taste for a bit of British machinery, not as pretentious as a Jaguar or the Rolls-Royce.

Martin Shaw's TV character Inspector George Gently drove a P5, then a P5B in the police series of the same name.

ROVER 3.5 LITRE COUPE

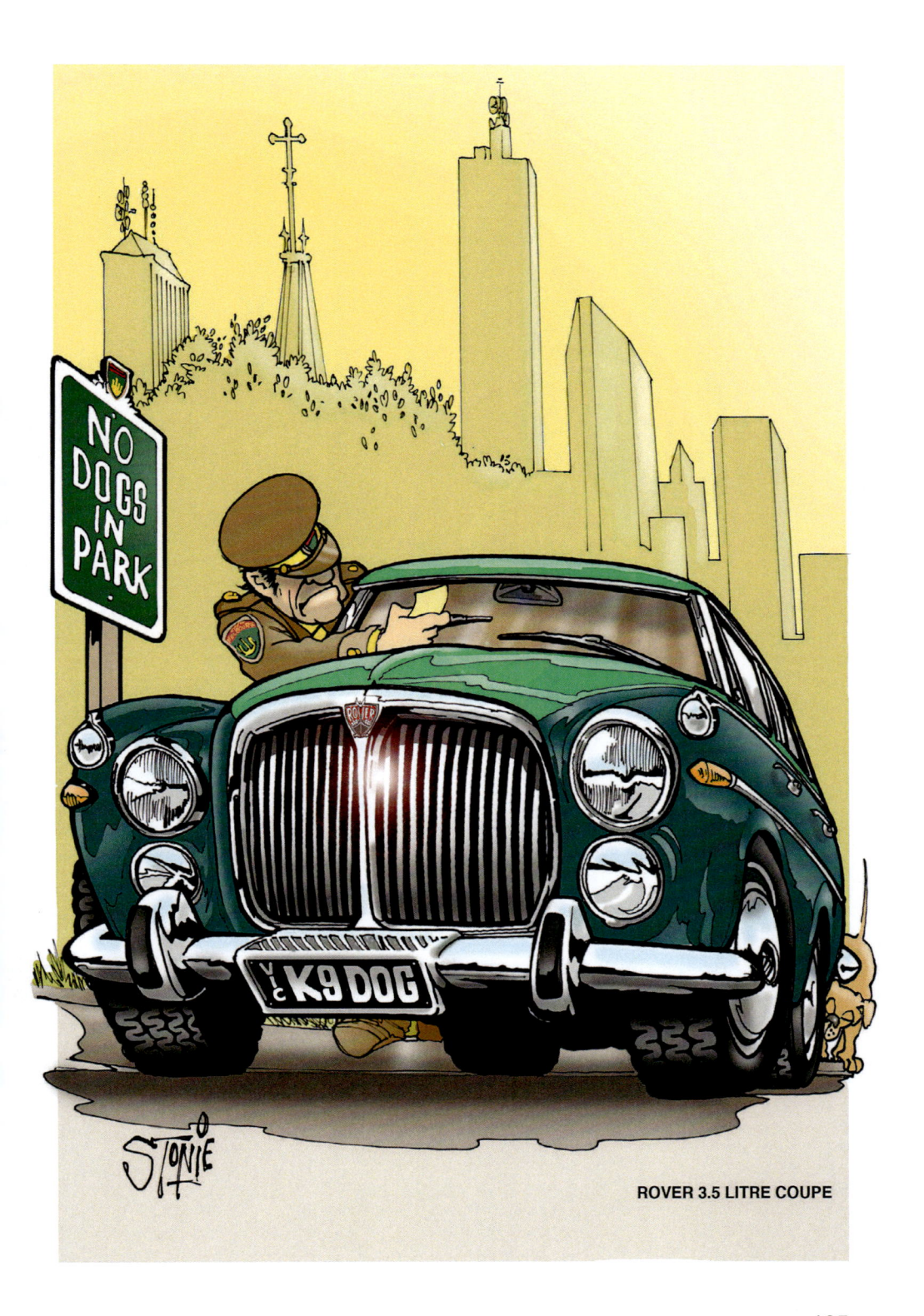

1913 Morgan Vee-Twin 3-Wheeler

"It can't make up its mind if it's a motorbike or a car!" A naff comment, as between wars many Brits could not afford cars, and a motorbike plus sidecar was the only transport that would fit the purse. The Morgan Car company hovered between the two, offering a relative level of safety and stability with their two seats, a windscreen, hand throttle and steering wheel.

The first agency to sell the Morgan Trike was Harrods department store, the only light cyclecar to appear in a Harrods window, at an appealing £65. You may be surprised that the Morgan three-wheelers excelled in the motorsport arena, winning trials and grand prix events like the 1913 Cyclecar Grand Prix at Amiens, France and the ACU Six-Day Trial in the sidecar class.

However their driver/rider, E.B. Wares, crashed and was badly injured racing a JAP-engined Morgan at Brooklands in 1924 and, as a result, three-wheelers were banned from car events. In 1927 Morgan Trikes won 11 Gold and 3 Silver at the MCC London to Edinburgh Trials.

By 1930, cheap four-wheeled microcars were flooding the market and the funny little Morgan lost market share. The last vee-twins had Matchless 990cc motors and most were shipped to Australia. Peter Sellers drove a Morgan three-wheeler in the opening scenes of the crazy 1968 movie The *Party*.

Harley-Davidson riders are rumoured to stop and take off their helmets for a Morgan three-Wheeler as it goes by, in honour of the origins of the vee-twin engine.

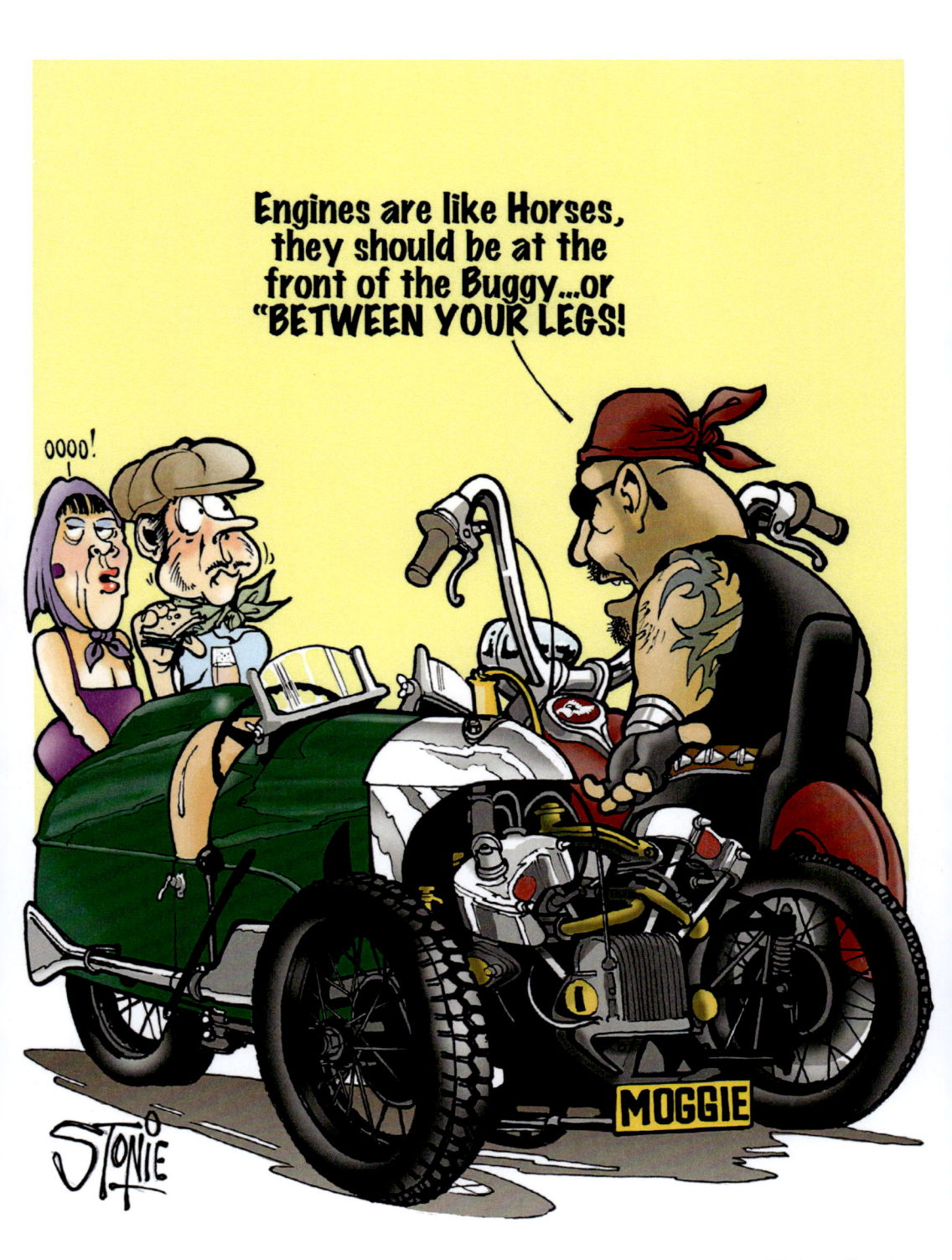

1926 Morgan V-Twin 3-Wheeler

The Bentley and the "Angle-Box"

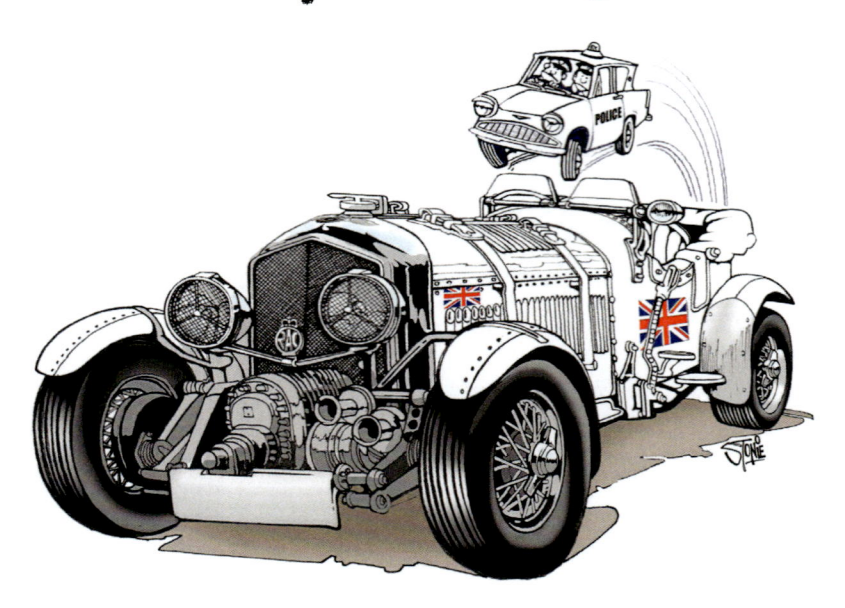

It's not possible to have a classic car book without an iconic 1924 Le Mans winning three-litre Bentley in it somewhere. Bentleys won the French classic race again in 1927, 1928, 1929 and 1930, with eventually a supercharged version. Ettore Bugatti allegedly said, "Bentley makes the fastest lorries in the world!"

Most of us have never driven and will never drive a three-litre Bentley but you would imagine you would need muscles like Mike Tyson and empty your bowels and stomach contents before you get behind the wheel.

The story of Walter Owen Bentley is movie material. Born to Adelaide, South Australian parents as one of nine children growing up in Hampstead UK, his engineering life started with Great Northern Railways in Yorkshire. After working with locomotives and racing motorcycles, he entered the motor vehicle industry, he innovated aluminium alloy pistons from an alloy paperweight.

In 1919 "W.O." and brother "H.M." formed Bentley Motors Ltd and started the legend of the famous "Bentley Boys" racers. Engineering was the cornerstone for W.O. but regardless of the wonderful aura of the Bentley name, a repetition of financial struggles sent this swashbuckling motorman selling out to and working for Lagonda, then Armstrong Siddeley and finally Aston Martin.

Married three times and with no offspring to follow on, W.O. was involved in the development of a new engine for the BMC Morris Minor which was his last daily drive.

The UK TV series *Heartbeat* was a passing parade of authentic classic cars, motorbikes, vans and buses. Visit the Goathland Heartbeat village in Whitby, North Yorkshire, and you may find the blue and white Ford "Angle Box" police car parked outside the general store. You might be lucky to see the occasional three-litre Bentley rumble by... but you will hear it first!

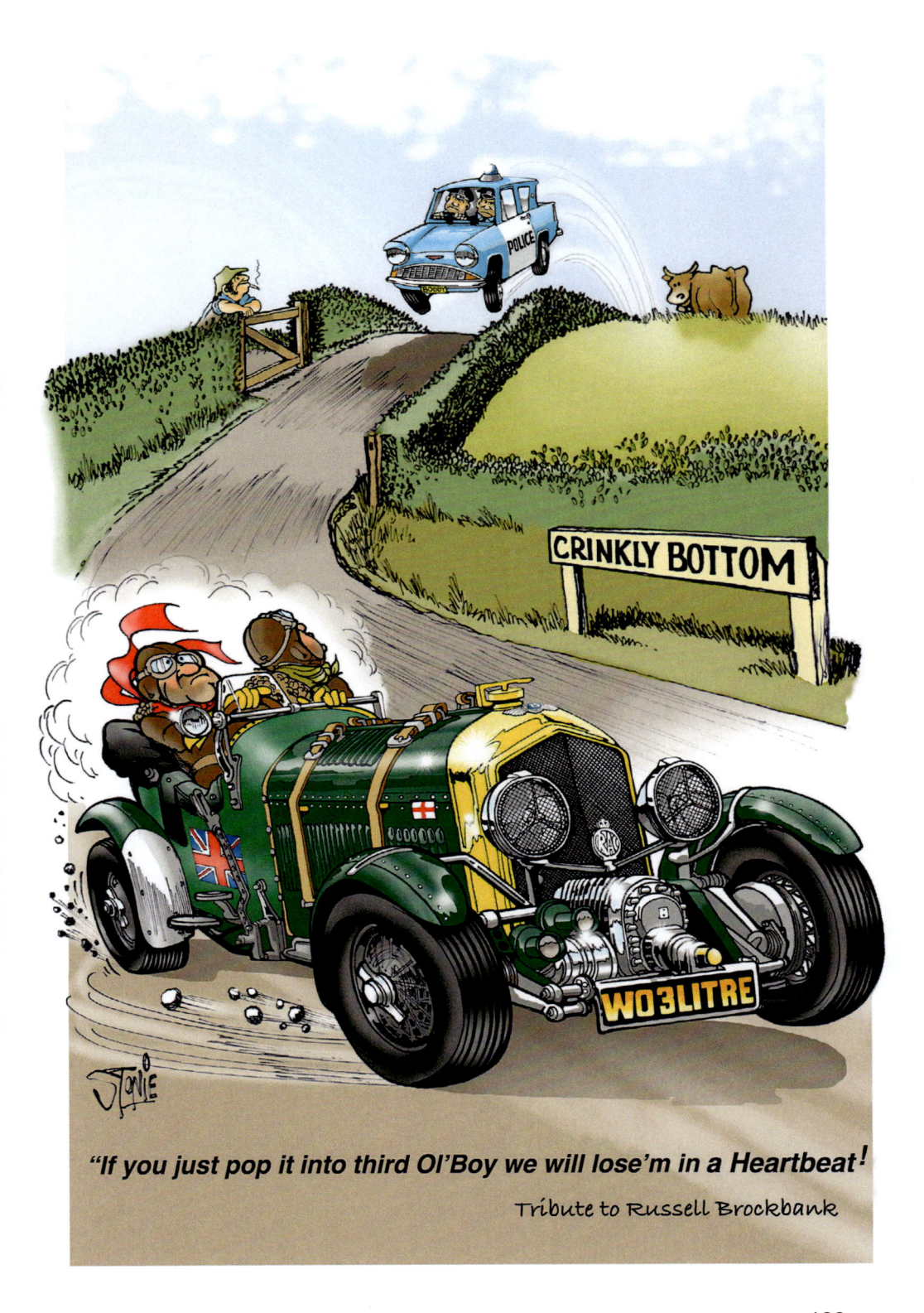

"If you just pop it into third Ol'Boy we will lose'm in a Heartbeat!"

Tribute to Russell Brockbank

1960 Chrysler New Yorker and the Drive

The Chrysler New Yorker was the name of the longest running production model in the USA from 1939 to 1996... almost as long as its body! This super city cruiser was as big a personality as the Big Apple and looked great in any colour as long as it was black.

Overshadowed by the super tail-finned Cadillacs and sixties' lifestyle, the *"New Yorker"* was an American motoring icon like the drive-in theatre. Firstly calling them "Park-In" movie parks, after serious development and research, Richard Hollingshead patented the drive-in concept and built the first drive-in theatre with individual speakers in 1933 at Camden in New Jersey USA.

You might say "Drive-Ins" went viral around Americanised countries because suddenly you could watch movies in the comfort (and privacy) of your car. Hollingshead's inspiration came because his mother endured skeletal pain sitting in a picture theatre, so he embarked on the idea of a drive-in movie park. From there drive-in everything became the norm, like Burger King and alcohol bottle shops, drive-in restaurants and drive-in banks...only in the US!

The drive-in had its teething problems, such as patrons driving off without putting the speaker back on its hook or falling asleep and getting locked in the park. The drive-in was also the ultimate dating site for teenagers and adults alike which contributed to a population increase.

One drive-in trick was to pay for two admission tickets with another four people crammed in the boot getting in for free. A Chrysler New Yorker was just the ticket for drive-in escapades.

The movie on the big screen opposite is *The Great (Car) Race* with Tony Curtis and Jack Lemmon.

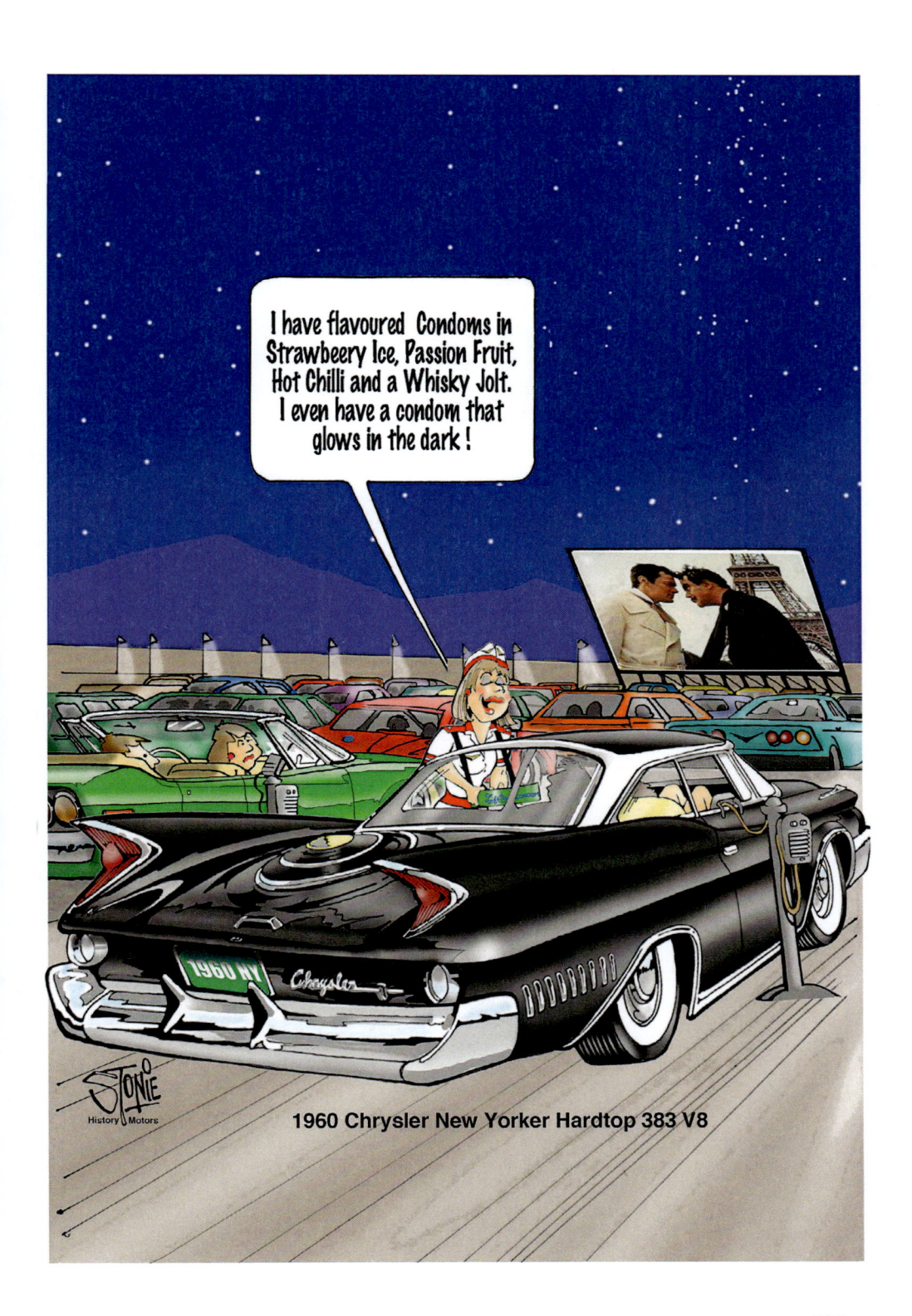

1960 Chrysler New Yorker Hardtop 383 V8

SHOW
PONIES

EXOTICAR ANNUAL
CONCOURS D'ELEGAN
He's not happy...
The Judge called it a Datsun
240Z kit-car !
LANCIA
MERCEDES-BENZ
JAGUAR
FACEL
VEGA
DO NOT
TOUCH
TOYOTA
2000
GT
1967
STONIE

133

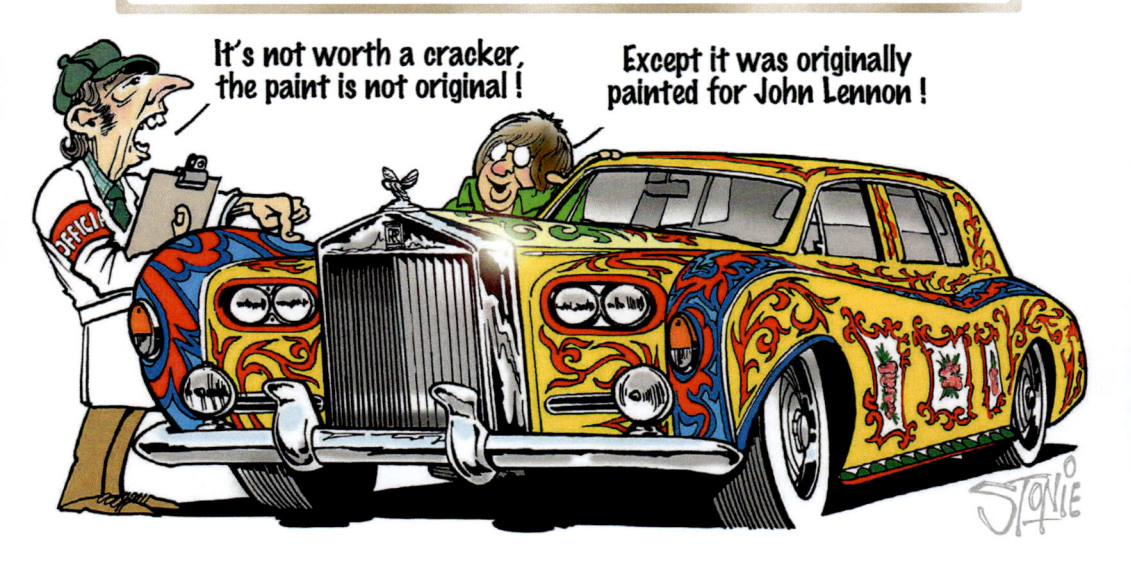

1929 Austin Seven "Chummy"

Sir Herbert Austin was the British Henry Ford when he explored the idea in 1922 of producing a light affordable car for the masses who could only afford motorbikes with sidecars. The Austin board members shunned the idea of a light car as company funds were all but gone. Acquiring the talent of a young draftsman, Stanley Edge, Herbert Austin designed their car in Herbert's billiard room at his Lickey Grange house.

After prototypes and design patents were done at his own expense, Herbert's Austin Seven was born. The company paid him £2.10 for every car sold. The Austin Seven saved the company. The motorbike and cyclecar market, however, was squashed. By 1930 290,000 Baby Austins had been produced. Multiply that by £2.10 and you do the sums.

Under licence BMW built the A7 as a Dixi while the French badged it as the Rosengart. Motor racing also promoted the Austin Seven. The 750cc sidevalve engine had a removable head and you didn't have to be a contortionist to give it a valve grind. It was so tough some Austin Seven racers were supercharged.

After World War II, the Austin Seven name lived on, even badged on the famous BMC Mini.

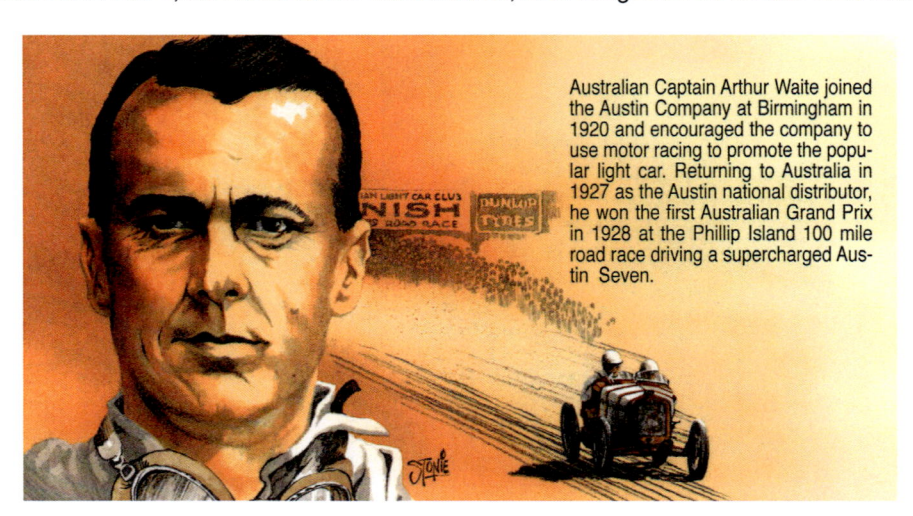

Australian Captain Arthur Waite joined the Austin Company at Birmingham in 1920 and encouraged the company to use motor racing to promote the popular light car. Returning to Australia in 1927 as the Austin national distributor, he won the first Australian Grand Prix in 1928 at the Phillip Island 100 mile road race driving a supercharged Austin Seven.

ORIGINAL CONDITION

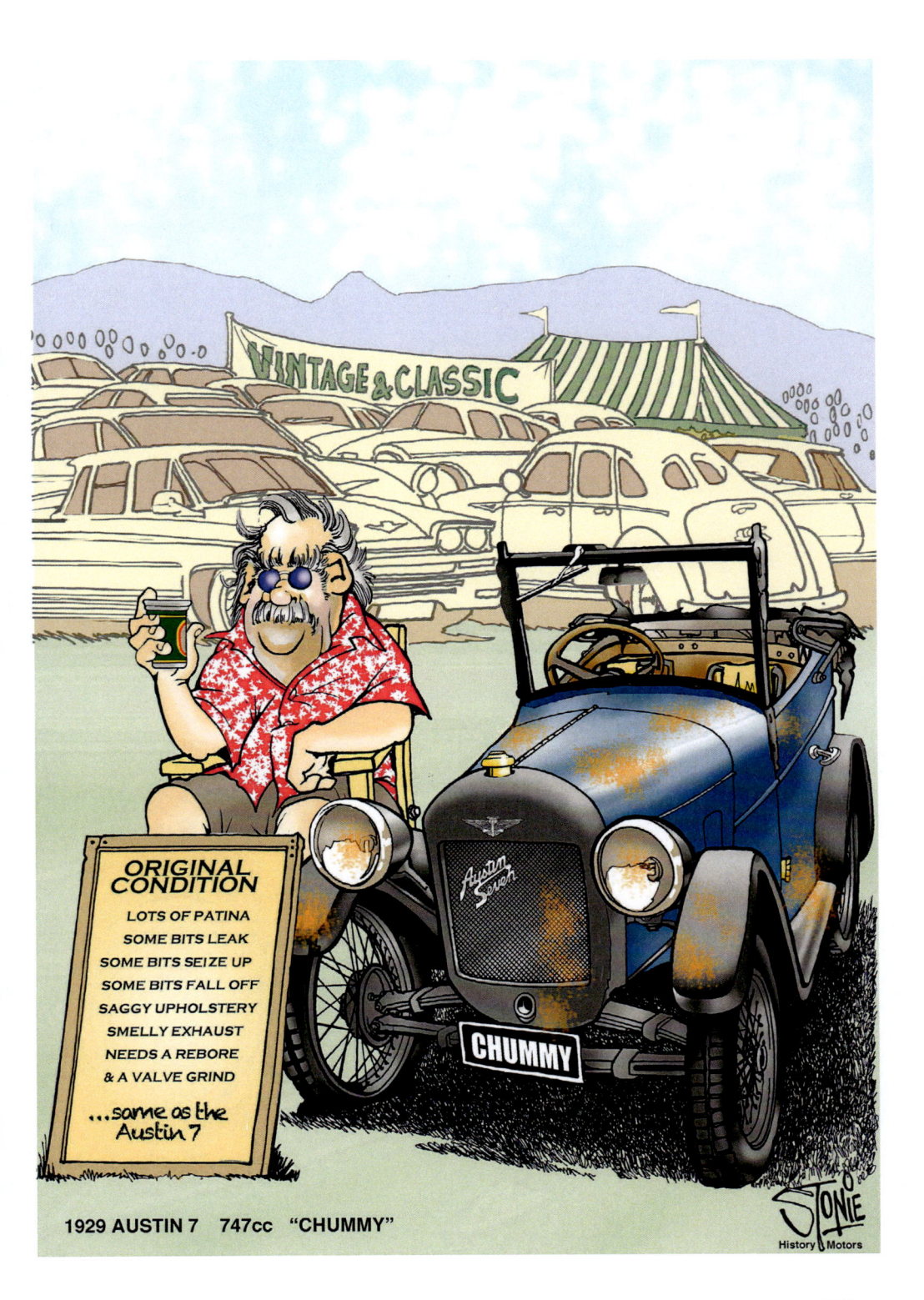

LOTS OF PATINA
SOME BITS LEAK
SOME BITS SEIZE UP
SOME BITS FALL OFF
SAGGY UPHOLSTERY
SMELLY EXHAUST
NEEDS A REBORE
& A VALVE GRIND

...same as the Austin 7

1929 AUSTIN 7   747cc   "CHUMMY"

135

1929 Roosevelt Marmon

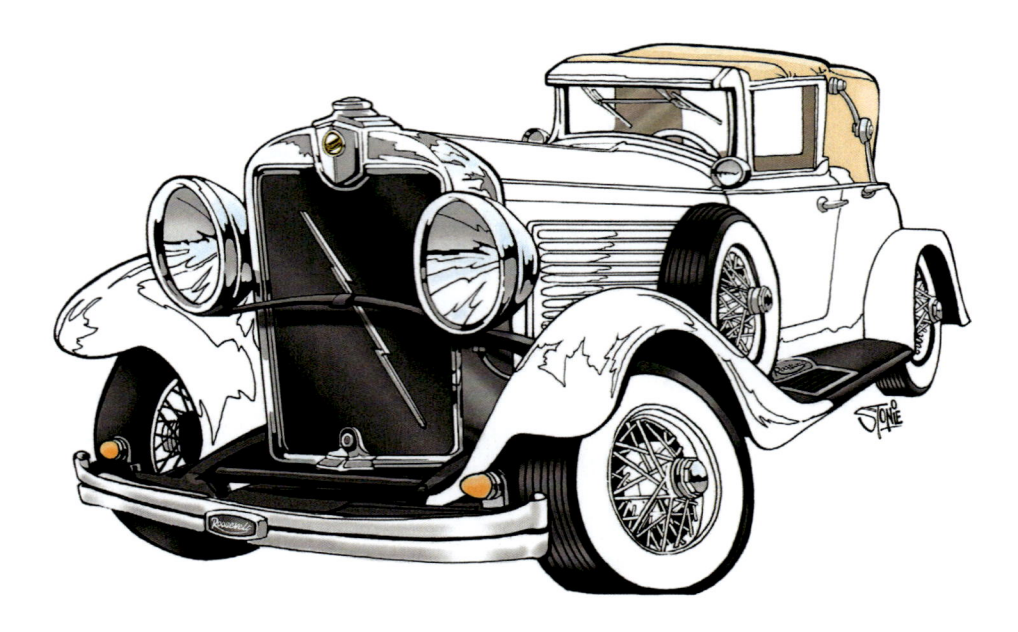

Well a "Betty Ford" or a "Rolls Reagan" never made the production line but a "Lincoln" certainly did. Few would have thought there was a car called a "Roosevelt" because it was a token gesture by the Marmon Car Company of Indianapolis and only lasted one year.

The irony of the Roosevelt model was that it ended the same year the stock market crashed in 1929. The Marmon Roosevelt was the first straight-eight-engined car in America apparently.

Marmon was also working on a huge V16 engine, the first in the world, but under severe financial struggles they were "Trumped" by Cadillac before it was finished in 1931.

The Roosevelt was designed to be the budget model for Marmon, priced under $US1,000. However if you were to try and purchase one of these rare production cars now, you may have to pay fifty times that.

Apart from being the first American straight-eight cylinder 202 cubic inch car, the Roosevelt had a horn button that could be pulled to start the engine and then twisted again to turn on the headlights. Ouch! You would not want to drink and drive.

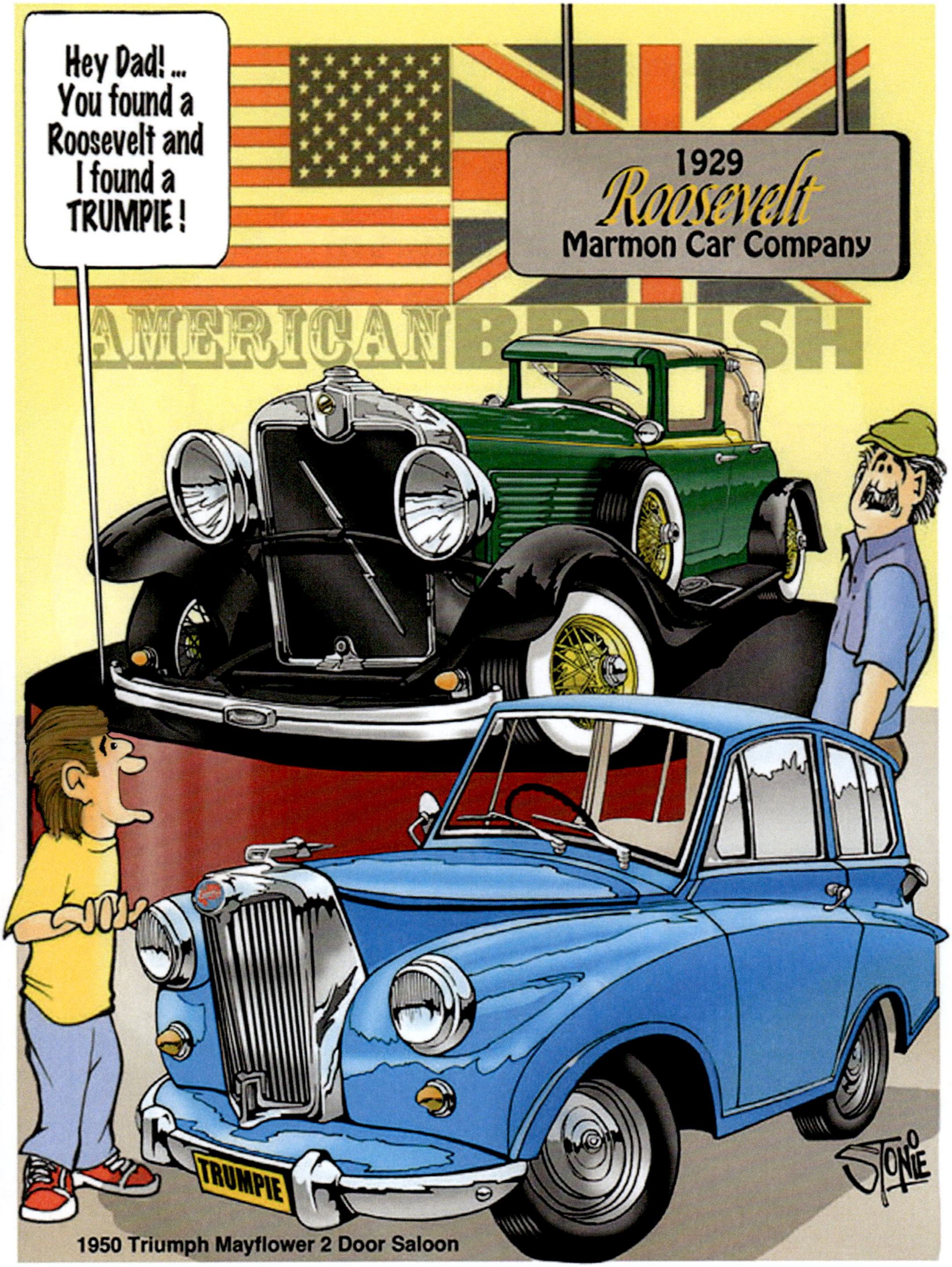

1950 Triumph Mayflower 2 Door Saloon

1962-64 Ferrari GTO 250

If you win the lottery and fancy buying a classic red Ferrari 250 GTO it will take your £30 million and your house, and you will have to sell the kids and put the wife on the street to pay for the maintenance and insurance. Why so expensive? Well, with Ferrari many models were shortlived and thus their value today is priceless, sayeth the Ferrarista.

In the sixties, Enzo wasn't really interested in the road-going cars except for the money he got from their sales to fund his Grand Prix team. However Mr Ferrari also presided over his American dealer, Liugi Chinetti, and often personally decided who could buy a new Ferrari sports car and who couldn't.

There were, of course, the Ferrari sports car teams that raced at prestige events like the Le Mans 24-Hour race and Daytona. Chinetti knew the value of racing the sports car versions as it turned over showroom sales, but, in order to beat the opposition, many models had a series of upgrades and short production runs.

It was boutique car-making at its finest. The iconic Ferrari GTO was built between 1962 and 1964. The 1962-63 cars were Series I, with an update in 1964 to Series II. From the outside, some came with a wide grille, then came the cat's-bum mouth grille, followed by the GTO with pocket ducts across the front of the engine hood. Some had two fender airflow slots, some three and four. Only Ferrari experts would know which is what as almost every car is different.

For us spectators... "Who cares, as long as it's red. Just start the thing up and let's hear that three-litre V12 engine sing above 4,000 revs!"

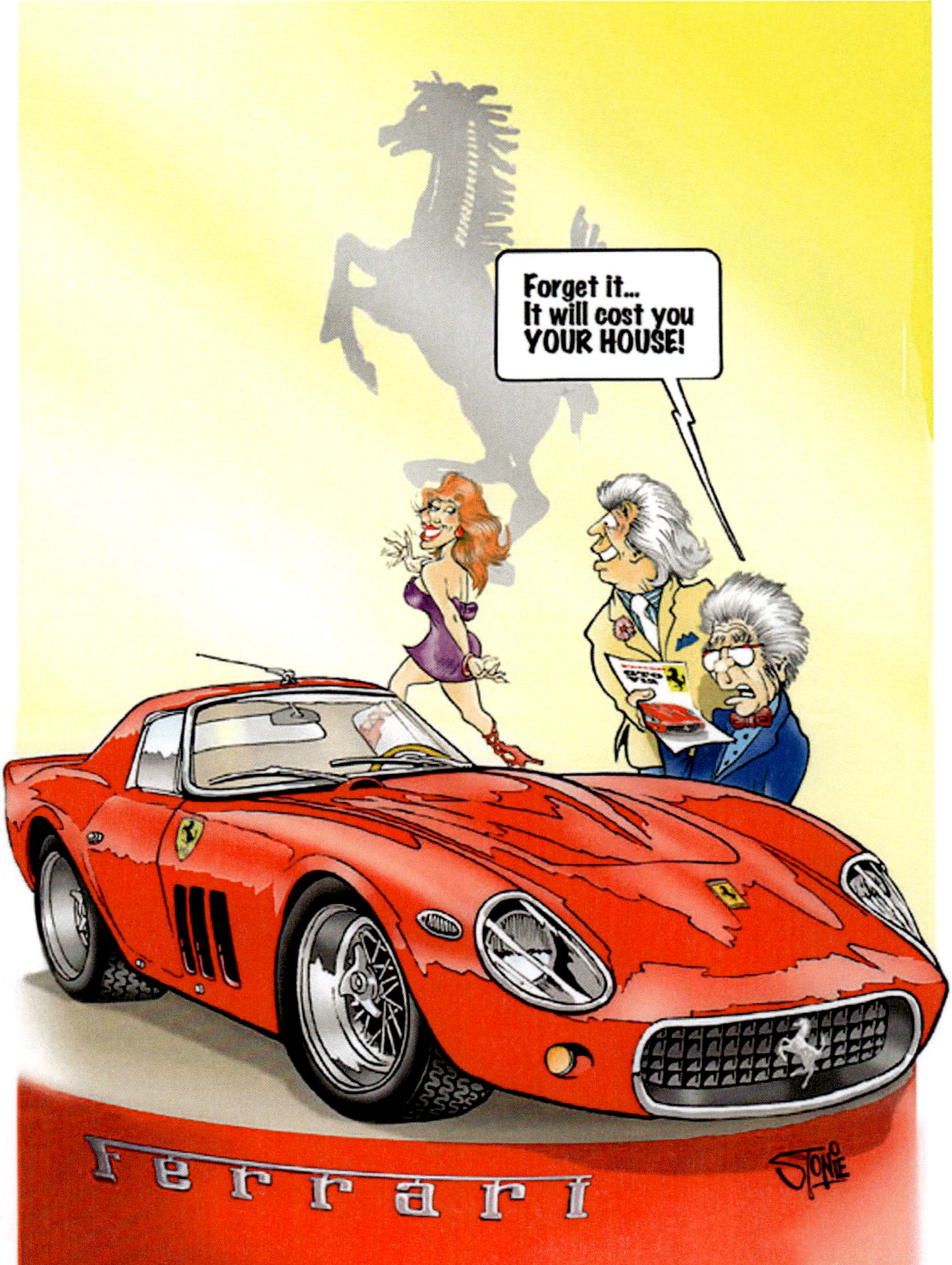
Forget it...
It will cost you
YOUR HOUSE!
Ferrari
STONIE

1960 Daimler SP250 V8

"It seemed like a good idea at the time," Daimler's second crack at a sports version after the Conquest model was the Daimler SP250. Called the "Dart" it was designed to lure American dollars, with a V8 engine and lightweight body style to get their attention. Well, it did in one way, as Dodge USA stopped Daimler using the name Dart because Chrysler Corporation had it registered as a trademark.

The Triumph chassis had a body made of some sort of glass fibre plastic. The initial motoring reports didn't match the sales brochures, but the alloy hemi-head V8 was reported as a 140mph projectile, providing there were no corners to negotiate. Daimler was eventually taken over by Jaguar and the SP250 was trashed.

However, while they weren't likely to use them as club racers, the British Police bought 30 black SP250 automatics, complete with a brass bell on the front, left over from the Wolseley Black Mariahs.

The Daimler SP250 was like a fifties' jitterbugger at a sixties' rock and roll dance. However, like all things from the past, sometimes they become more popular as classic masterpieces in retro, like old has-been one-hit wonder rock stars.

Classic car collectors who like oddball motoring marques always find a unique reason for owning a car like the Daimler SP250 Dart, if only to pose down the motorway at a lazy 100mph, with that smooth Daimler 2.5-litre V8 throbbing noise, with the roof down and the radio on playing *Apache* by The Shadows or the Ventures version of *Walk Don't Run*.

1960 Daimler SP250 V8 unofficially known as the Dart

Datsun 240Z & Toyota 2000 GT

Few automobile designers would dream that one of their keynote designs would have two bites of the cherry, a Japanese Fuji Cherry no less. Count Albrecht von Goertz, an American-German designer, attracted the Japanese industry's attention because of his elegant design of BMW's 507 sportscar. Now, it may sound confusing, but Nissan asked Yamaha to design a new model of its 2000 sports car and Goertz was commissioned to do a sports coupe design that would appeal to the Americans. Nissan shelved the design owned by Yamaha but later offered it to Toyota who were also looking to do a sports coupe.

Toyota, often referred to as a white goods car maker, saw the design as a new image for them. They called in Satoru Nozaki, their own designer, who came up with a limited edition alloy body idea having pop-up headlights and a cockpit for Japanese legs. Satoru San was an E-Type fan and the Toyota 2000GT got some Japanese artistic licence.

Convertible?...? Well, yes, referring to the 2000GT in the James Bond film *You Only Live Twice*. That was one of two made for the film because Sean Connery's six-foot frame didn't fit in the cockpit of the coupe, so they cut the roof off.

Toyota only produced some 340 2000GTs and, while not having quite the value of Ferrari limited editions, a nice clean 2000GT fetches a very pretty penny these days.

Meanwhile, back at Nissan, their US dealers changed their mind and wanted to go ahead with a coupe sports car. Whether they saw the familiar-looking Toyota 2000GT or just remembered Herr Goetz's original coupe design, somehow it found its way back to Nissan. This time, Yoshihiko Matsuo, head of Nissan's styling department, put his own spin on the body shape for the sports coupe.

The big plus with the Yoshihiko Datsun coupe design was that it had more room for long American legs. In unison, the Japanese Fairlady was built at the same time as the American version, but the US Samurai was launched a month before the Japanese model. There was a rumour, up to the launch in the US, that they still didn't have a name for the US coupe and the Japanese obsession for the movie *My Fair Lady* didn't sit well with the American Nissan dealers.

At the last minute, it was badged as the Datsun 240Z, denoting the 2.4-litre straight-six engine. Tokyo was shocked but cooled down when 156,076 cars sold in the first year, making the Datsun "24 ounce" an overnight market leader around the world.

I don't care who designed which car first... you didn't save me any of my favourite sushi !
WORLD AUTO Designers SHOW
BRISTOL 404 Coupe
KARMANN
DATSUN 240Z
S30 Original design by Albrecht Goertz Final by Yoshihiko Matsuo
DATSUN
2000 GT
TOYOTA 2000GT
2000GT
Original Design by Albrecht Goertz US-German Finished design by Satoru Nozaki
TOYOTA
STONIE

1948-58 Land Rover Series I

Maurice Wilks lived in North Wales and had an old army Jeep on his farm in Anglesey. He also happened to be the chief designer for the Rover Company. The carmaker had been bombed out of their own factory during the war and moved into an old Birmingham aircraft factory. After 1945, everything was taxed or rationed to pay back the Americans for winning the war.

Wilks' farming experience gave him the idea to produce a utility vehicle for the farming community, inspired by what the Standard Car Company was doing with its Ferguson Tractor. Based on his old Willys Jeep, he designed a simple-bodied light-agricultural small truck made from alloy, because there was a tax only on steel. He also fitted the Rover P3 1.6-litre engine to minimise the tax on fuel efficiency.

The P3 four-speed box was fitted with a two-speed transfer box which meant the 4WD setup also had a free-wheel action which allowed rear-wheel drive. Full four-wheel drive was operated by a ring-pull lever under the dash. There was a power take-off on the front to operate farm machinery. The new utility was half the size of a light truck and half of a tractor, perfect for post-war farmers.

The body colour was only ever going to be ex-army surplus green which was cheap, with plenty of gallons available. The Land Rover was launched at the 1948 Amsterdam Motor Show, where it was an astounding success. Who would have thought that even a new Queen of England would ride in a specially built "Royal Landie".

Seventy years later these alloy-bodied farm trucks have become a collector's item: 70% of old Land Rovers are still working today. As the British farmer became wealthier, a demand arose for a more luxurious version than the basic cheap jeep style.

After that the Land Rover had to be reclassified from a commercial vehicle (free from purchase tax) to a proper road vehicle. Then much later came the "créme de la créme", the Range Rover!

LAND ROVER 250 SERIES 1 1954 CORONATION TOUR

1954 Facel Vega Series II

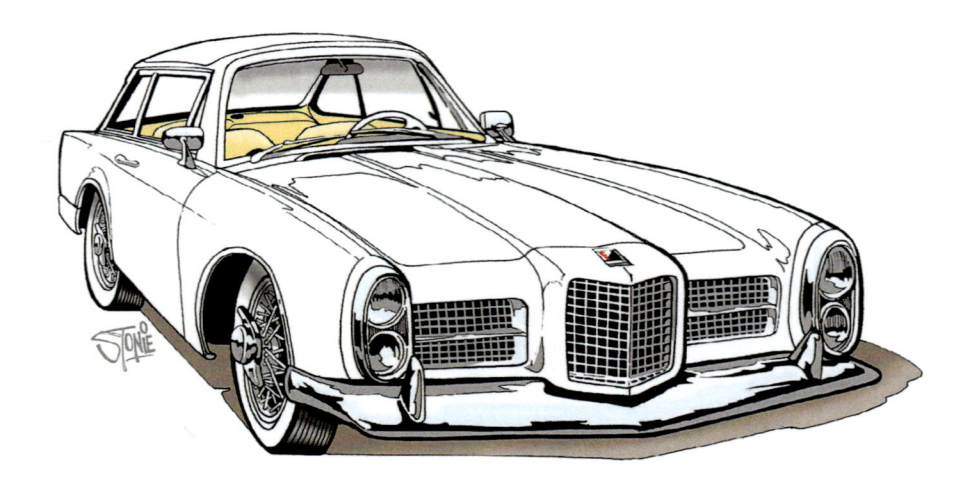

When you think of French cars, Citroëns with air-bag suspensions, Peugeot rally cars and racing Renaults come to mind, all with small bore screaming engines and funny gadgets. Not so the Facel Vega!

The French heavy metal pressing company, Facel built boutique bodies for other automobile makers like Simca, Delahaye even Ford of France, pressing bumpers, hubcaps and grilles.

When monocoque one-piece, non-chassis car bodies came into fashion, Facel lost most of its main manufacturing income and decided to build its own luxury car for the upper classes, the opposite of what other French carmakers were producing.

The 1954 Facel Vega HK500's huge two-door coupé design was a muscle car with a Chrysler 4.5-litre V8 under the hood and trimmed to appeal to a lavish taste. Aimed squarely at the American market, loaded with French panache and avoiding the heavy French horsepower tax, the US target market was a bullseye, with most Facels exported to the lavish land of America.

Film celebrities such as Joan Fontaine, Danny Kaye, Tony Curtis, Ava Gardner and even the Beatles' drummer, Ringo Starr, loved owning a piece of elegant French thunder. Picasso thought it a motoring masterpiece and had to have one. They naturally featured in a few movies.

Upgrades in 1956 to a 5.4-litre and later again to a 6.3-throbber made the 1962 Facel Vega Series II lighter and faster. A four-door model was added with the popular two-door coupé and yes, there were a few convertibles.

The only scary component of the early Vega was the four-wheel drum brakes which couldn't stop this rolling mass, so the introduction of four-wheel Dunlop discs made the top speed of 140mph a little safer. Driving in a Facel Vega is like driving your lounge room around!

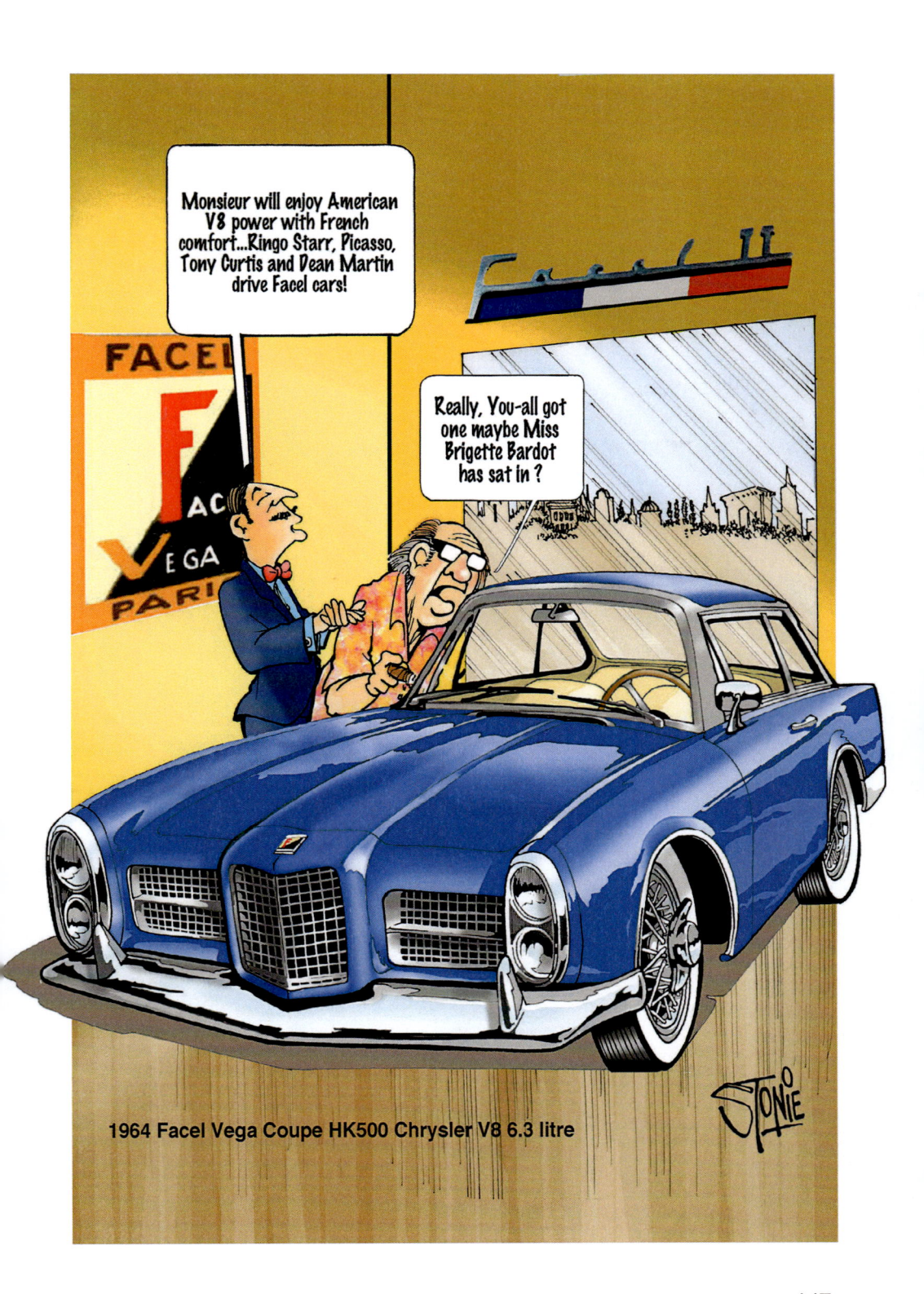

1964 Facel Vega Coupe HK500 Chrysler V8 6.3 litre

THE WEIRD
THE "WHY"
& THE
"WHAT FOR?"

WHAT... We can't come into Italy because we have five people in an Audi Quattro? I WANT TO SPEAK TO YOUR SUPERIOR !!!
Sorry, eez busy with two people in a Fiat Uno !
HALT !
SWISS
ITALIAN
BORDER
STONIE

OH MAN !... I gotta' get me one of theeese !
TAR BRUSH
PUSS
STONIE

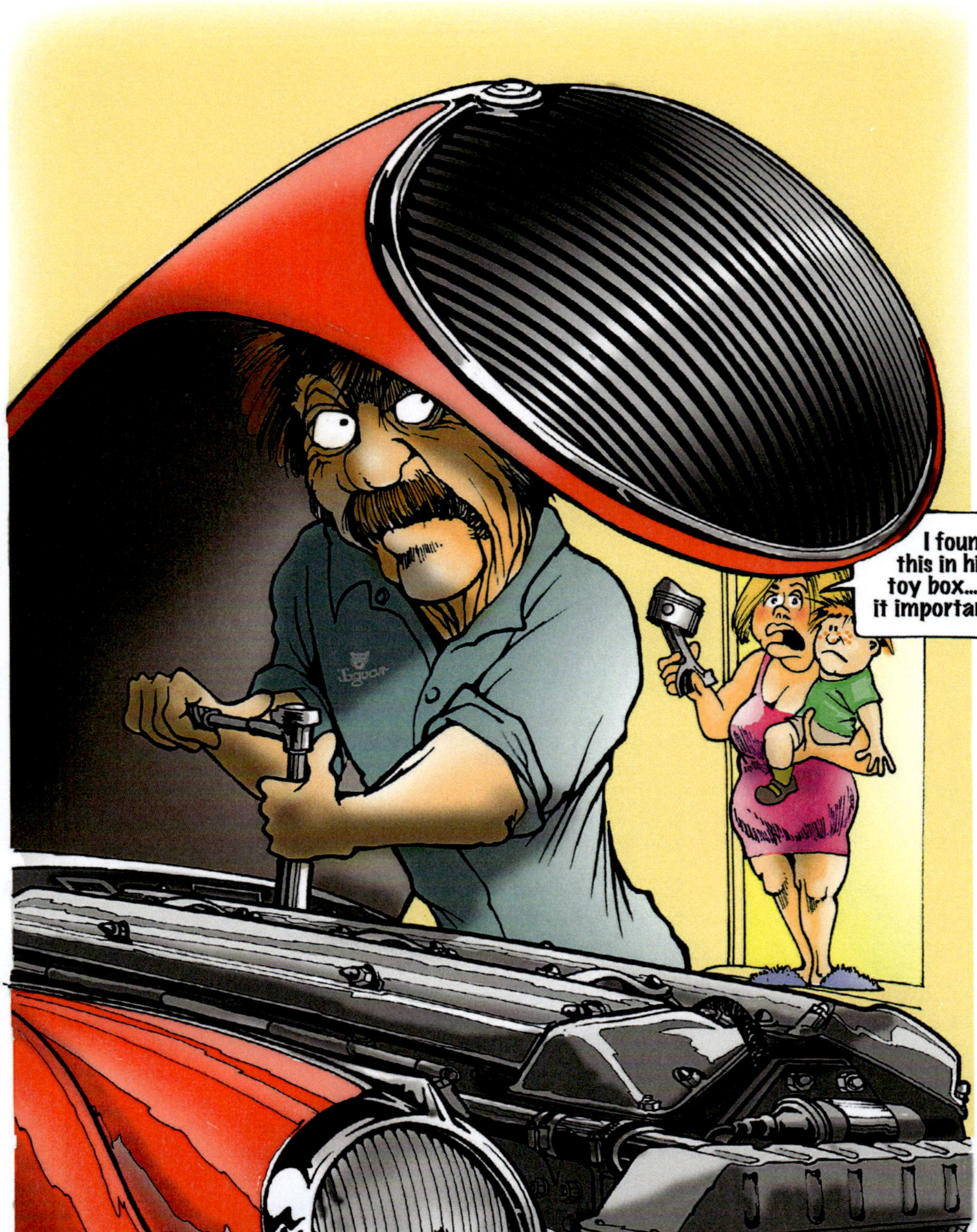
I found this in his toy box... is it important ?
Jaguar

1928 Chevrolet National 4

During WWII the British fighter plane the Spitfire was referred to as "the Rolls-Royce of the skies" and the American/Commonwealth P40 Warhawk/Kittyhawk as "the Chev of the skies". The Spitfire upgrades and changes were so numerous that maintenance and refits were a nightmare, as new spare parts would not fit earlier models. The Kittyhawk however was easy, as old parts and new spares all fitted, so the P40s were far easier to keep flying. Chevrolet cars and trucks carried a similar reputation in the motor industry.

Louis Chevrolet, co-founder of the Chevrolet Motor Company in Detroit in 1911, was a Swiss engineer and racing driver. William Durant, who would team up with young Louis Chevrolet, used him to race GM Buicks as a promotional exercise.

Later Durant offered up Chevrolet Cars to worm his way back into General Motors as president, but was sacked again so GM kept the "Chevy" name to launch motor cars designed to suit buyers "for every purse and purpose".

Interestingly, later, the US Automobile Association ruled out car manufacturers being directly involved with motor racing and GM were the only ones who stuck to the agreement removing the racing image of Chevrolet.

The 1928 Chevrolet National 4 replaced the Chev Capital and this low-revving (2000rpm when cruising) 2.8-litre four-cylinder "war hawk" with a four-wheel braking system, chugged its way into the hearts of America and everywhere else in the world, launching the Chevrolet brand as reliable people transport. The bow tie Chevy badge became as recognisable as the Ford oval.

It was, however, well-advised when cranking this big four to be careful of the kick-back if it didn't start on the first turn, as it could easily break your arm! It is believed recipients of the crank handle coined the word "cranky" when the car wouldn't start.

1928 CHEVROLET NATIONAL FOUR

1949-61 Morris Commercial J-Type Van

"I want one!" a remark every kid in the neighbourhood would say when the Morris J-van replaced the horse-drawn deliveries of bakers, milkmen and bottle'os.

The double sliding doors meant milkies and bakers could quickly leap out and make their drop-off deliveries with ease. Many a van-man would come back to his J-van and find a local kid sitting in the driver's seat, the Morris J-van being so cute every kid thought he could drive one easily.

This 1476cc sidevalve-engined Morris Commercial could be ordered in many different coachwork configurations and was a popular import to many British Commonwealth countries. The British Mail versions had a rubber suspension to give a softer ride for the posties and in 1957 the upgraded JB van had an overhead-valve engine and went to a four-speed shift. By 1961 some 48,600 J-vans had been produced.

One advantage the horse-drawn carts had was a very important attribute, the horse. Dear old Dobbin remembered when to stop at all the houses that were on the delivery list.

One tall tale of the horse-drawn delivery days was that of a baker who was having an affair with the lady at her house and while he would dash in for a quickie, the horse would continue on down the road, obediently stopping at each house. A dishevelled baker was often observed running after his cart!

"Gee those warm buns we pinched out of the driverless cart tasted good!"

1949 MORRIS J TYPE VAN

1959 Firebird III "Blister" Prototype

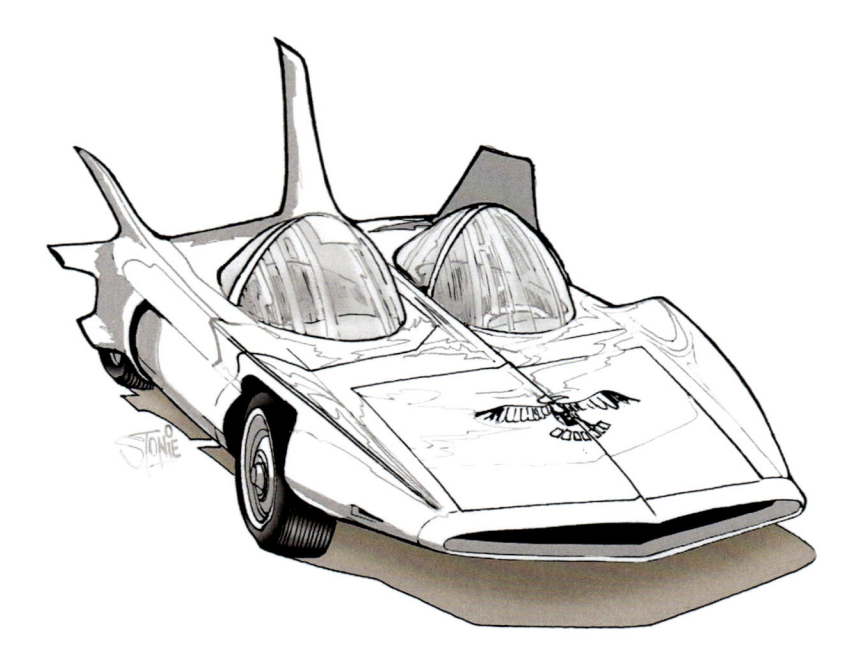

General Motors' legendary automobile designer, Harley Earl was a great fan of aircraft, rockets and spacecraft design. He was also the father of the General Motors road-going Motorama motor show.

The designers were all keen to come up with a weird car design for the Motorama show but Mr. Earl was hard to beat.

All jokes aside, what these designers were doing was clairvoyancing the future car not unlike the solar, electric and driverless prototypes today. General Motors' design team used gas turbine power and or fibreglass bodywork with aerodynamic wings as air brakes to help slow these sonic boomers from an estimated 200mph.

At the end of the 1950s, Firebird III had wild accessories like anti-lock brakes, cruise control and no-hold steering automated guidance systems. At high speeds there was an ultrasonic device that opened the doors to brake the speed down.

Whoa! Probably a good thing some of these rockets were for show only and never tested, as getting sucked out of the car at 200mph would not end well.

Harley once lived next door to Cecil B. De Mille in Hollywood and often visited the film sets. He got the idea of using film set clay to model car designs which became the norm for car design models worldwide. Living next door to Cecil B. de Mille is why Earl's obsession with fins and wings was bigger than *Ben Hur!*

A chrome model of the Firebird I sits on top of the Harley J. Earl Trophy that is presented to the winner of the Daytona 500 car race every year.

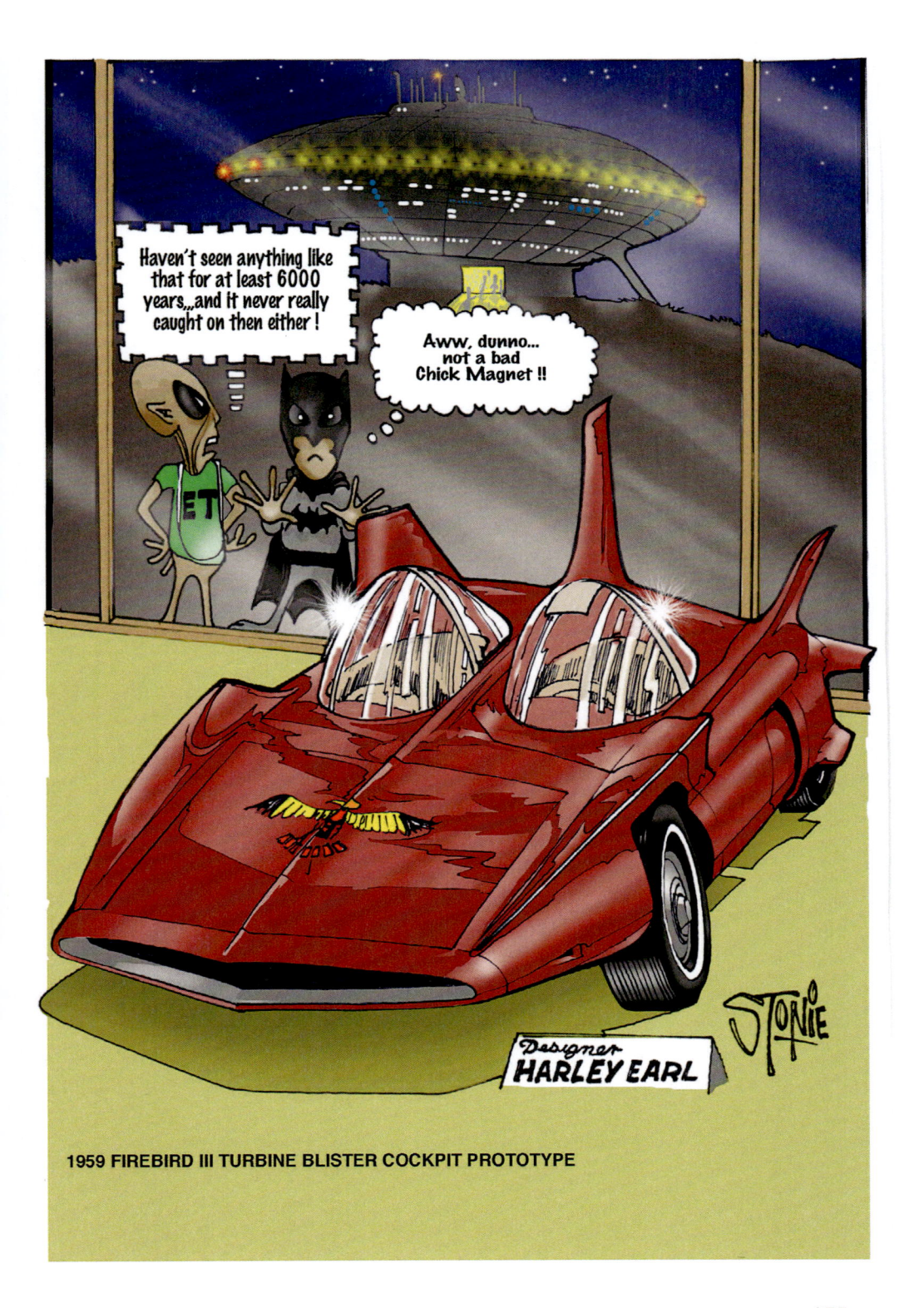

1959 FIREBIRD III TURBINE BLISTER COCKPIT PROTOTYPE

The Anderson Detroit Electric Car

The urban legends of oil moguls murdering inventors who came up with an alternative to the internal combustion engine are unfounded (we hope). Many inventors had similar stories to Donald Healey (of Austin Healey fame) who invented a 200mph steam car which, it's rumoured, North Sea Oil bought the patent for and buried it. Many stories like that are bandied around the dinner table.

During the First World War, Anderson Electric Cars were selling 1000 to 2000 units a year due to the high price and restrictions on gasoline. Often described as a "lady's car" because these battery-electric carriages didn't need to be cranked, is maybe why Disney cartoon character Grandma Duck drove something that looked like an Anderson. Actually it was a 1914 Baker Electric Car.

In 1920 the Anderson name became the Detroit Electric Car Company and between 1907 to 1939 some 13,000 electric cars were sold.

It's interesting the notable people who owned an Anderson Electric Car like Henry Ford's wife Clara, Mamie Eisenhower, Thomas Edison and John D. Rockefeller Junior were owner-drivers.

Many countries are intending that, by 2040, internal-combustion-engined cars will be banned. Manufacturers like Audi, Volvo, BMW and Mercedes-Benz are planning to release production electric cars by 2030. General Motors' Volt plug-in electric cars passed 100,000 sales in 2016.

What on earth will the politicians and civil servants tax with the loss of their life-pension revenue scrounged from petrol?

1915 ANDERSON ELECTRIC CAR - DETROIT

1948 Chevrolet Fleetmaster Woodie Wagon

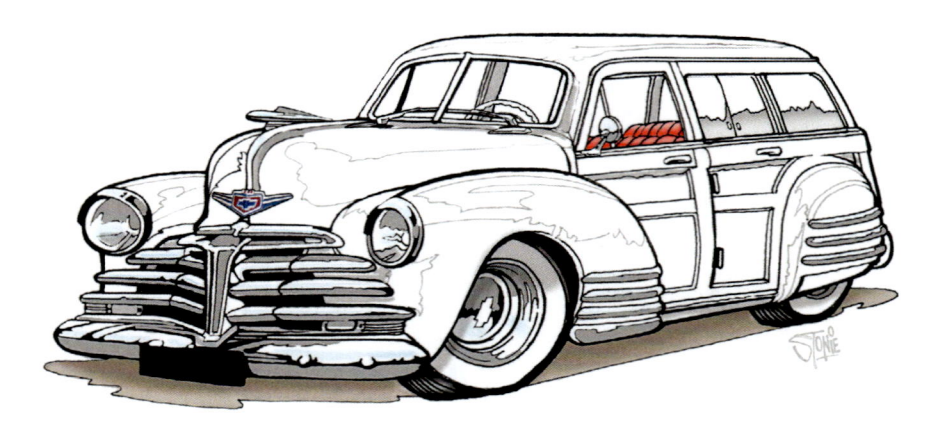

Every surfer in the mid-fifties aspired to having a Chevy woody wagon to stack the surfboards out the back window and head down the coast to chase waves. Maybe they thought because of the wood it wouldn't rust from the sea spray like a normal car.

The 1948 Chevrolet Fleetmaster woody cabin area was just about all wood, the floor of the wagon was flat wood, the roof lining had slats along the top and the tailgate and door panels were wood-lined. Today a 1948 Chevrolet Fleetmaster woody in top condition will cost you a cattle ranch.

The woody wagon (estate and traveller or station wagon by some marques) became a fashion symbol for the country farmer and ranch owner, but why did they use wood really?

Maybe they were limited edition models and the wood panels were easier to build than tooling up pressed-steel specials. The craze spread not only to all American carmakers, but across the Atlantic too.

The 1950s' Healey Elliott had a woody model, and Morris Minor and Morris Oxford had the wood estate included in their model range. However in the sixties when they wanted to do a BMC Mini woody van they found it way too expensive to produce for a limited demand.

The ultimate woody was a 1930 Rolls-Royce Phantom II Estate which appeared in a *Miller's Collectable Price Guide (2003/4)* that had suffered a rust problem with its fabric-covered panels and the woodwork replacement served as a better option for the handsome £60,000 Roller.

Ford Australia produced a 1963 Falcon XM Squire station woody wagon but the panels down the sides were plastic! Well, they didn't rust! The Falcon Squire production lasted maybe two years. Would you believe they are worth good money if you find one where the plastic hasn't cracked and fallen off. Only in "Osstrailya".

1969 PORSCHE 912 2 LITRE 4   1948 FLEETMASTER CHEVROLET "WOODIE"

1969-72 Holden Torana GTR & XU-1

The Australian Torana model started as a British General Motors Vauxhall Viva which was so underpowered, you had to change down a gear in a headwind! However, Formula One world champion "Black" Jack Brabham once put a Coventry Climax engine in a Vauxhall Viva and in Australia there was a thing called a Brabham Torana with twin carbies. A Mini Cooper it wasn't!

General Motors-Holden Australia had a problem as Ford Australia was dominating the famous local mountain circuit, the Bathurst 500-mile production car race...and selling cars very well from their many victories. General Motors America never had a motor racing policy, so the Holden dealers got together and funded a racing programme to beat Ford on the track and in the showrooms.

"Torana" is a local indigenous people's word meaning "to fly" and the Holden dealers led by Harry Firth built a homologated limited edition Torana GTR LC model with a hot six-cylinder engine and strong gearbox to race up against the V8s.

The styling was Opel/Vauxhall with a long almost Pontiac nose but what went underneath the skin was the trick: the triple Stromberg, 2.8-litre straight-six engine with limited-slip differential. So the XU-1 LJ version became the giant killer and Holden Torana won the Bathurst 500 in 1972.

When the General Motors Detroit executives arrived in Australia and wanted to see the so-called experimental Firth workshop, Harry would take all the wheels off the race cars and fit winter-tread rally tyres and tell the GM heavyweights they were rally cars. It worked, as did the racing success for both Holden and Ford's policy of "Race'm on Sunday, sell'm on Monday".

1969 HOLDEN TORANA LC GTR

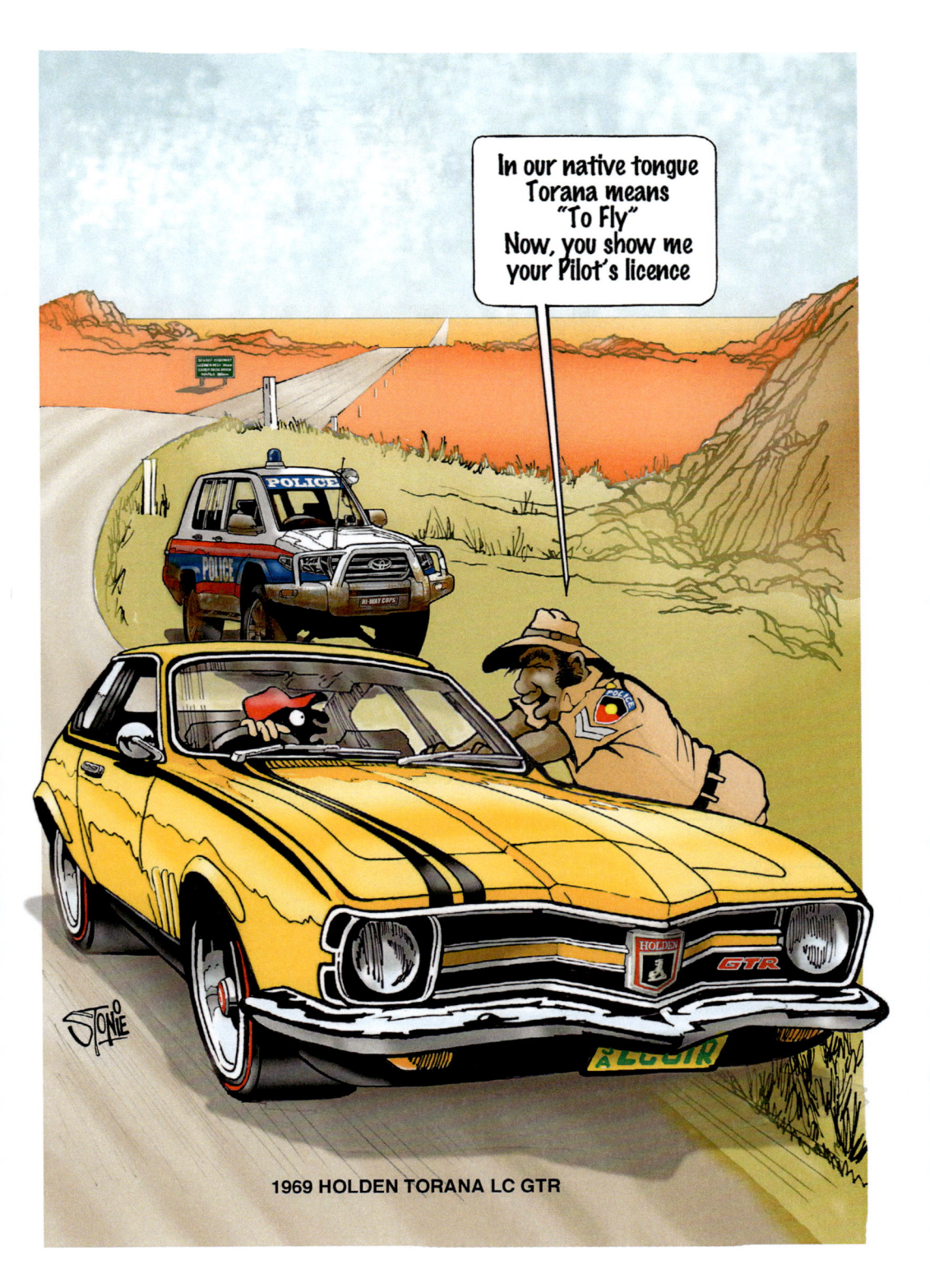

1938 DKW 700cc Twin Utility

Perhaps better known for its motorcycles, DKW (Dampf Kraft Wagen meaning "steam-powered car") also produced affordable pre-war cars and imported derivatives from a knock-down base to car builders/fabricators to many points of the globe including Australia. The simple front-drive twin-cylinder two-stroke scavenger engine was a great workhorse in dry, sandy, arid conditions (like Australia).

With a simple gravity-feed oil-fuel supply and a dynamo-starter-generator electric system, the "Deek" proved reliable and the drivetrain remained cooler in hot conditions whereas similar petrol-engined cars failed in the Aussie sun. The oil-fuel mix two stroke had a good even torque response and the central dash-mounted gear lever was a very cute French touch.

Maybe the front transverse springs needed attention regularly as the spring bolts would work loose and steer the car like a shopping trolley. The DKW's wood chassis meant it was never used during WWII so it's amusing to see a DKW in a modern war movie.

"Das Kleine Wunder" (the little wonder) was a nickname that lived with DKW from 1919 when the company made tiny toy engines for models. DKW, merged with Horch (meaning "Listen!"), Audi (also meaning "Listen!" but in Latin) and Wanderer companies, to form Auto Union and the four-circle-badge is still used on Audi cars today.

After the war, DKW continued to make cars and their small bore saloons were an economical high-performing touring car, regularly raced.

1938 DKW AUTO UNION CONVERTABLE UTILITY

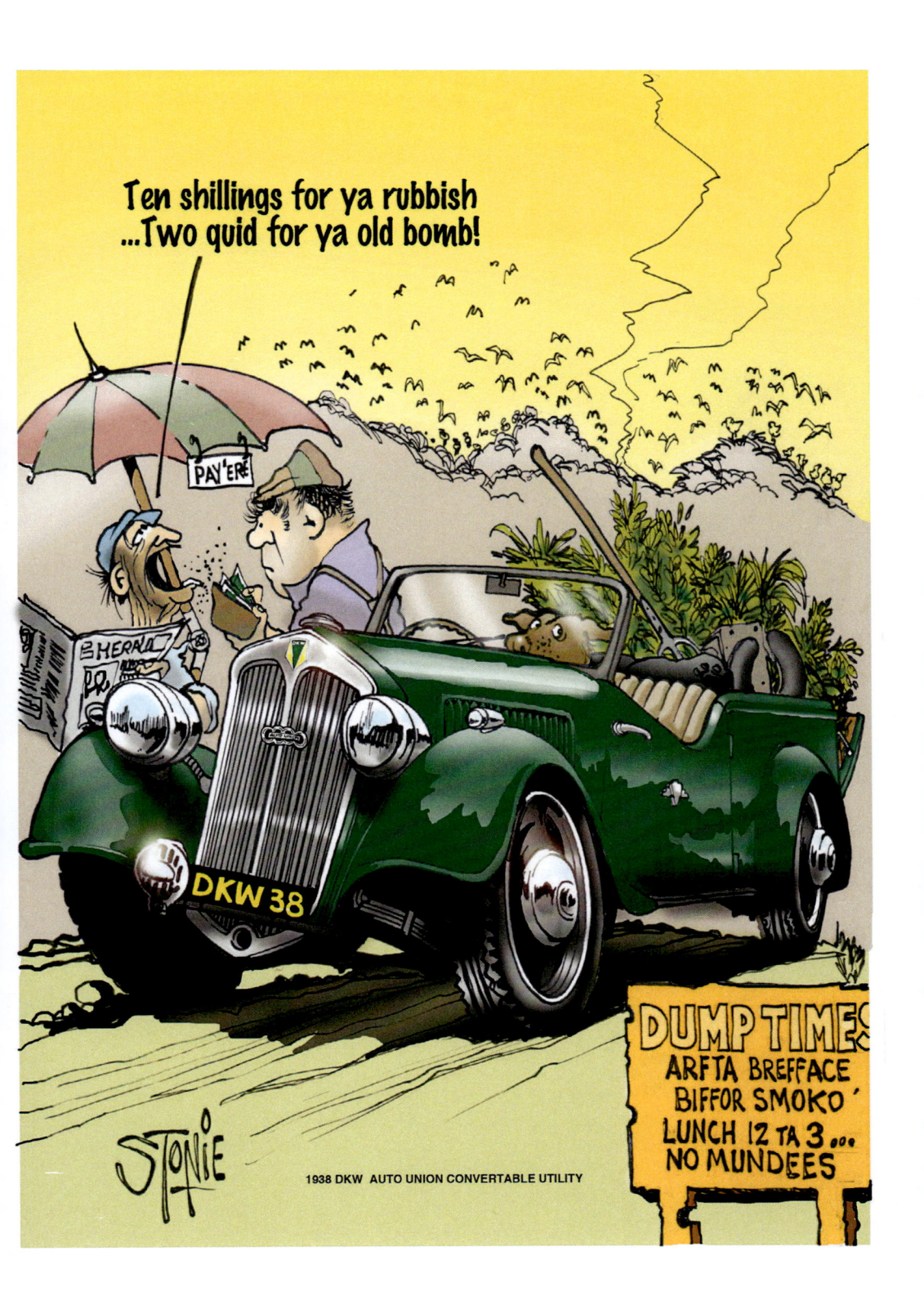

1941 Willys/Ford "Jeep"

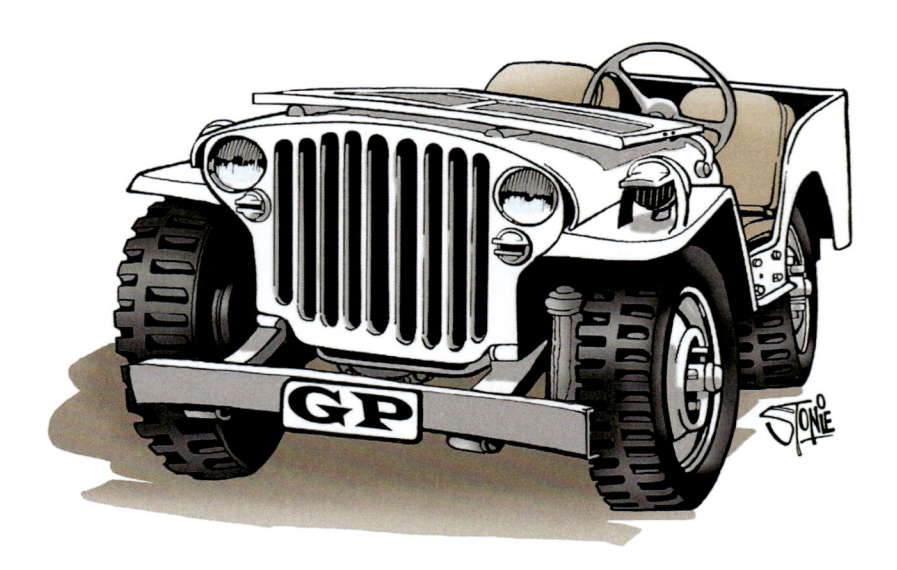

The war in Europe had already started when the US Army called for lightweight vehicle prototypes for all-terrain purposes. Car manufacturers went to work, but the key was going to be who had the capacity to keep up the production demand. When it got down to three manufacturers, they all went into production with a US Army schedule which meant working night and day.

Bantam Car Company was the first unable to keep up the schedule. Willys' MA model was doing well and the troops loved the powerful four-wheel drive all-terrain "buggy" that was a hoot to drive. Willys were struggling to keep up the build demand so Ford was contracted to build the popular Wiilys model in tandem. Ford called its model GPW, the W for Willys. Willys produced 363,000 and Ford 280,000.

So..what's in the name? Most believe "GP" meant general purpose and "GeePee" got shortened to "Jeep" but history says "Jeep" or "GP" was already a common name for some US army trucks. Doesn't matter...the Jeep culture just would not die, because this was such a unique vehicle, living on through the Daimler Chrysler Jeep era and now under the Fiat brand.

An interesting anecdote in slot-grille history is that the Willys/Ford GPW Jeep nine-slot flat grille design is as famous as the Rolls-Royce grille. It is alleged that Ford still owns the trademark nine-slot grille.

The new Chrysler Jeeps were not allowed to use nine-slots so they shortened them to seven. Just to ruffle the history books a bit more, the Ford-owned nine-slot Jeep grille trade mark also applied to the Hummer which uses a version of the seven-slot grille only because of a technical oversight by DaimlerChrysler.

A real Willys/Ford Jeep, fully restored in army green with MASH logos, will always turn heads on the streets.

1942 Willys MB JEEP 4cyl. 3 Speed

1929 Hudson Super Six

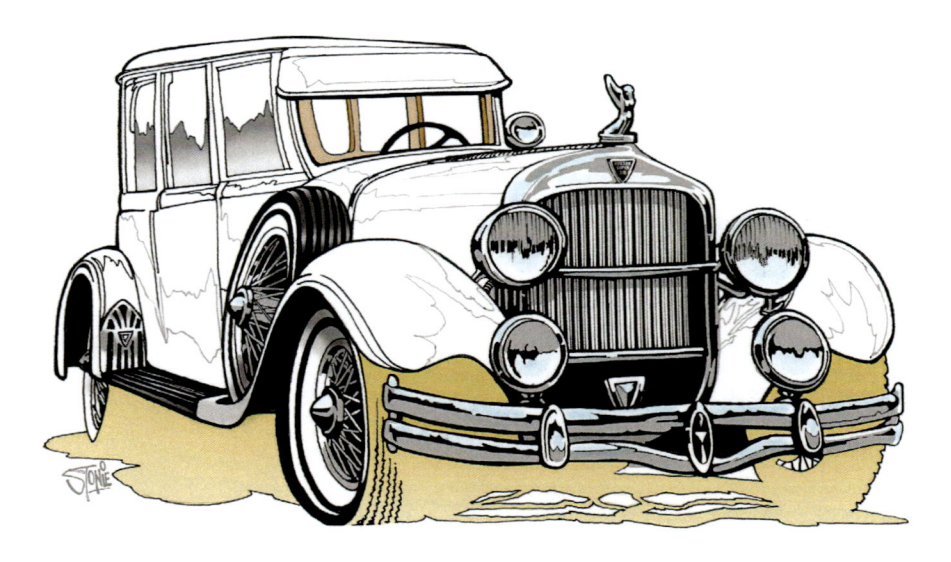

The Roaring Twenties produced plenty of material made into movies, mostly about gangsters in big luxury cars that all looked the same in box-shaped coachwork and vertical grille design. However, under the bonnet things often got clever and the Hudson Super Six was just such an automobile.

The Super Hudson had a different application for operating the intake valves on its flathead engine with a push-rod action while the exhaust valves were the same as on a normal flathead. Hudson owners say the smooth power is comparable to bigger and more powerful cars.

A 288 cubic inch engine with 6:1 compression ratio plus a thing called an accelerator pump helps the 92hp pull this huge saloon which is not stressed about cruising all day at 70mph (110km/h).

Can't find any figures on a torque rating, but sounds like it could easily pull the back axle out of a police car with a chain. All it needs is a Thompson machine gun on the front seat next to the driver.

The Hudson has starred in movies and TV shows the likes of *Danger Ahead* 1929, *The Thin Man* 1934, *Dillinger* 1973, *Bullets Over Broadway* 1994 and the Australian TV series *Miss Fisher's Murder Mysteries 2014*

1929 HUDSON SUPER SIX   1958 FORD ESCORT POLICE VAN

1960 MGA Twin Cam & 1966 MGB

After the classic sweetheart MG TF, Morris Garages needed to attack the market share of the Austin Healey and develop a new modern rounded body shape sports car. Using the traditional soft top & side curtains and no visible door handles was always going to be very acceptable to MG enthusiasts.

The gobsmacking launch of the MGA with three racing-prepared roadsters at the 1955 Le Mans 24-Hour Race was a masterstroke. Although the '55 Le Mans race suffered a tragic crash with a Mercedes killing 84 spectators, the MGA went on to be a success. MG didn't rest on their laurels, they released a coupé tin-top version with front disc brakes and engine increase from 1500 to 1600cc. In 1957 yet another brave model released was a twin-cam version with four-wheel discs, close-ratio gearbox and centre-lock steel wheels!

The "A-Type" was a huge success out-selling the combined total of all other sportscar makes. Unfortunately the twin cam had generic engineering problems which needed re-tweaking by specialist tuners. However, as the 100,000th MGA rolled off the line, its replacement was announced at the same time: the MG "B".

This new model did not go down well with the MGee-hardists. Shock horror! It had wind-up windows and gadzooks, it didn't have a chassis! To this day the various MG registers in the powerful worldwide club say the MGA was the last "real" MG. But for the well-informed, the B is a well-balanced sports car with bags of legroom, 1800cc engine with nice torque (95bhp) and speed (easily 110mph).

If you chopped it in half down the middle, you would see a design where the engine, the cockpit and fuel tank sat in a well-thought-out body. They even had two six-volt batteries, one behind each seat.

Aaah! Then the bean counters ran out of production money and it suffered 1954 lever-action front shockers and leaf springs on the rear. The three-bearing motor was upped to a five-bearing and the gearbox later had synchromesh on first, plus an electric overdrive in 1968 which made it a pleasant long-range touring roadster.

MG realists will say the three-bearing was a bit quicker than the five and collectors can pick a five-bearing with push-button door handles rather than lever-action handles on the three-bearing model.

The MGB sold its doors off and for the non-wind-in-the-hair enthusiast came a delightful hatchback MGBGT. Though not recorded, Pininfarina designed the roof and hatchback. An unpopular, front heavy MGC Healey-six-engined, understeering model followed with a bonnet hump. This was followed by the MGBGTV8 with the longest initials for a car in history. The Rover 3.5-litre V8 killed the big C six because it was lighter and had fabulous torque!

Where did you find these barn-MGs?
BARN-CAR SHOW
WINNER 1st
SECRET SHED CARS
Si...Mexico!
HOSE B
HOSE A
1960 MGA TWIN CAM 1966 MGB
STONIE

1928 Willys Falcon Knight Roadster

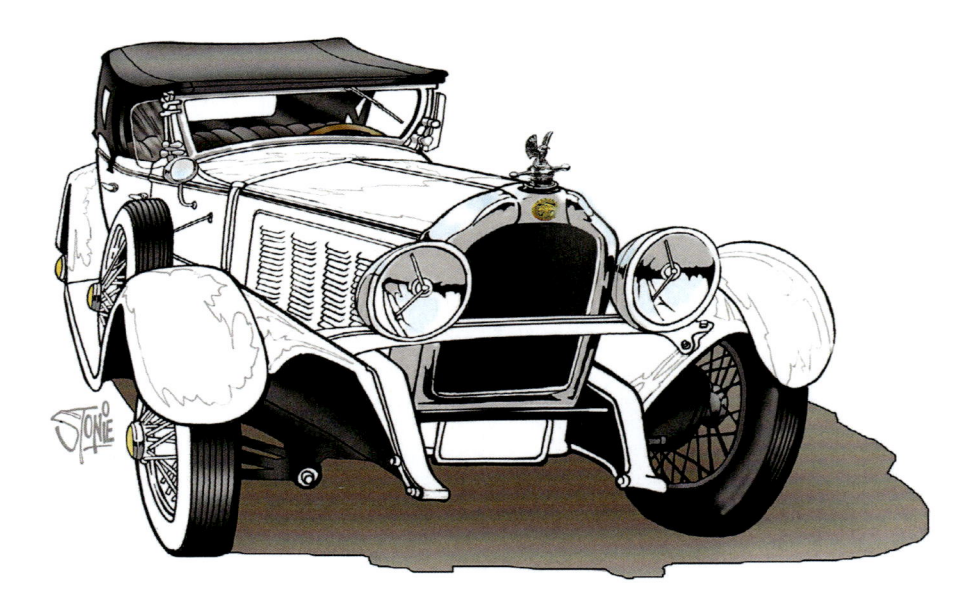

An automobile called a Falcon should have been as common as a Mustang and the logical radiator emblem would have been a bird of prey in flight, but the first Falcon was the Knight. Willys had moved from Long Island NY to Toledo Ohio and developed the Knight sleeve-valve four- and six-cylinder engines. The flagship model in 1927 was the Falcon sedan, luxuriously appointed. Later the favourite model was the Roadster.

There it was, the Falcon radiator cap emblem perched on top. The Willys Company had even registered a separate company, the Falcon Motor Corporation and made the car in a truck factory elsewhere in Ohio. The whole operation came to an end in 1929 and the Falcon name was dead.

Ford popped up in 1960 with a compact lightweight six in two and four doors but the pick there was a two-door hardtop lightweight Sprint version.

The scuttlebutt was that Chrysler US was about to put the Falcon badge on its new compact model, but Ford had registered the name just six hours before Chysler headed for the registrar's office. Instead Chrysler used the name Valiant on its new compact car.

The Ford Falcon compact was also made in various forms in Canada, Australia, Mexico and Argentina. Ford Australia's 1970 Falcon GTHO 351cui V8 was the fastest four-door saloon car in the world and won the 1970 and '71 Bathurst 500 production races at the Mount Panorama circuit.

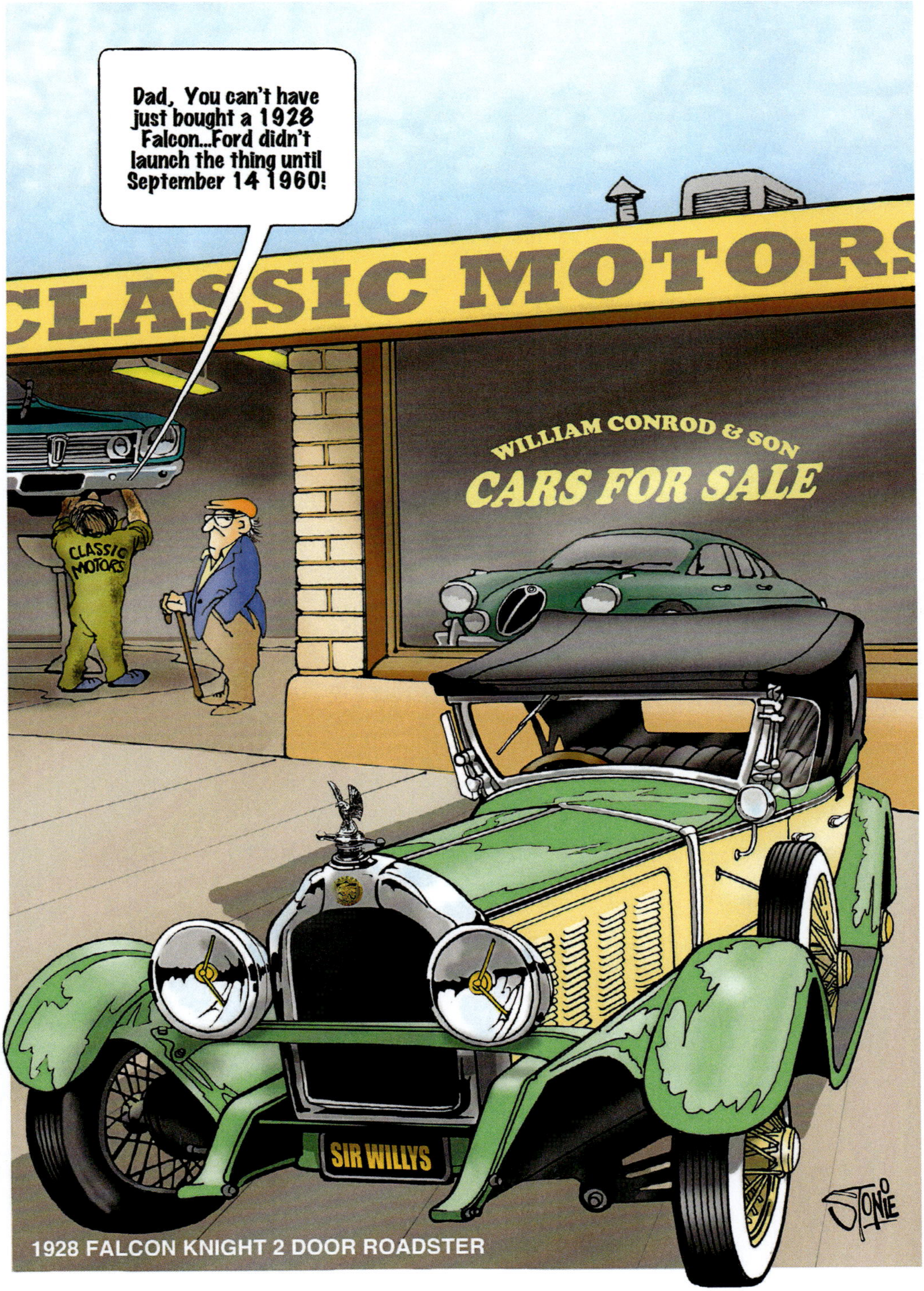

1928 FALCON KNIGHT 2 DOOR ROADSTER

1966 Aston Martin DB6 II Volante

Product placement in the James Bond movies to the later major sponsor deal with the 2018 Red Bull Formula One Team are not the only reasons Aston Martin is the prince of promotion in placing its cars on the world stage.

The decision of His Royal Highness Prince William to borrow his father's royal blue Aston as a going-away conveyance at his wedding in 2011, was the greatest promo for Aston Martin worldwide.

This was a great break from tradition for the British Royal family when you consider their motor garages were full of Rolls-Royce limos and horse-drawn carriages designed for normal royal events.

The "royal" Aston Volante (Italian for flying) was such a cool look for the young royals right down to the number plate "JU5T WED" using a "5" as the "S", typical of William and Kate's cool personas with a loyal public.

The DB6 was a 21st birthday present to Prince Charles from Her Majesty Queen Elizabeth II. In keeping with his environmental projects, Prince Charles had Aston Martin restoration expert, R.S. Williams, convert the DB6 to biofuel.

The removed alloy pistons and steel conrods did not go to the tip. Instead two editions of cufflinks were crafted for charity. The DB6 Series II is Aston Martin's longest-running model production to date.

1966 ASTON MARTIN DB6 "ROYAL" VOLANTE

1934 Ford Utility V8 "Kangaroo Chaser"

Henry Ford was asked if the people demanded the production of the T-model. "No!" he said. "If I asked the people what they wanted, they would have said, give me a faster horse!"

However, one thing he didn't give them was a modern light packhorse. It was those pesky Australians who say they invented the all-steel-bodied utility, the "ute"! An Aussie farmer's wife wrote to Ford Australia complaining that when they went to church on a rainy day in the open-sided ragtop pick-up, she got wet!

The letter was passed onto the design department and then to a 22-year-old design student, Lewis Bandt. Lew thought by using a saloon body he would chop off the roof at the back from the B pillar and make an open-tray area using the sides of the saloon, putting a tailgate on the back panel for easy load access.

The cabin was completely weatherproof with wind-up windows, so when the farmer and his wife went to town to take livestock to the market, she could wear her Sunday best. Ford Australia built 500 of them, thus the Aussie ute was born.

Later, Lew was sent to Rouge River, Detroit, USA, with two examples of the Aussie ute to show Henry Ford and, when he called in his executives to see the Australian derivative, they asked, "What the hell is that?" Henry replied, "It's a kangaroo chaser!"

Lew Bandt's 1934 40A Ford Utility

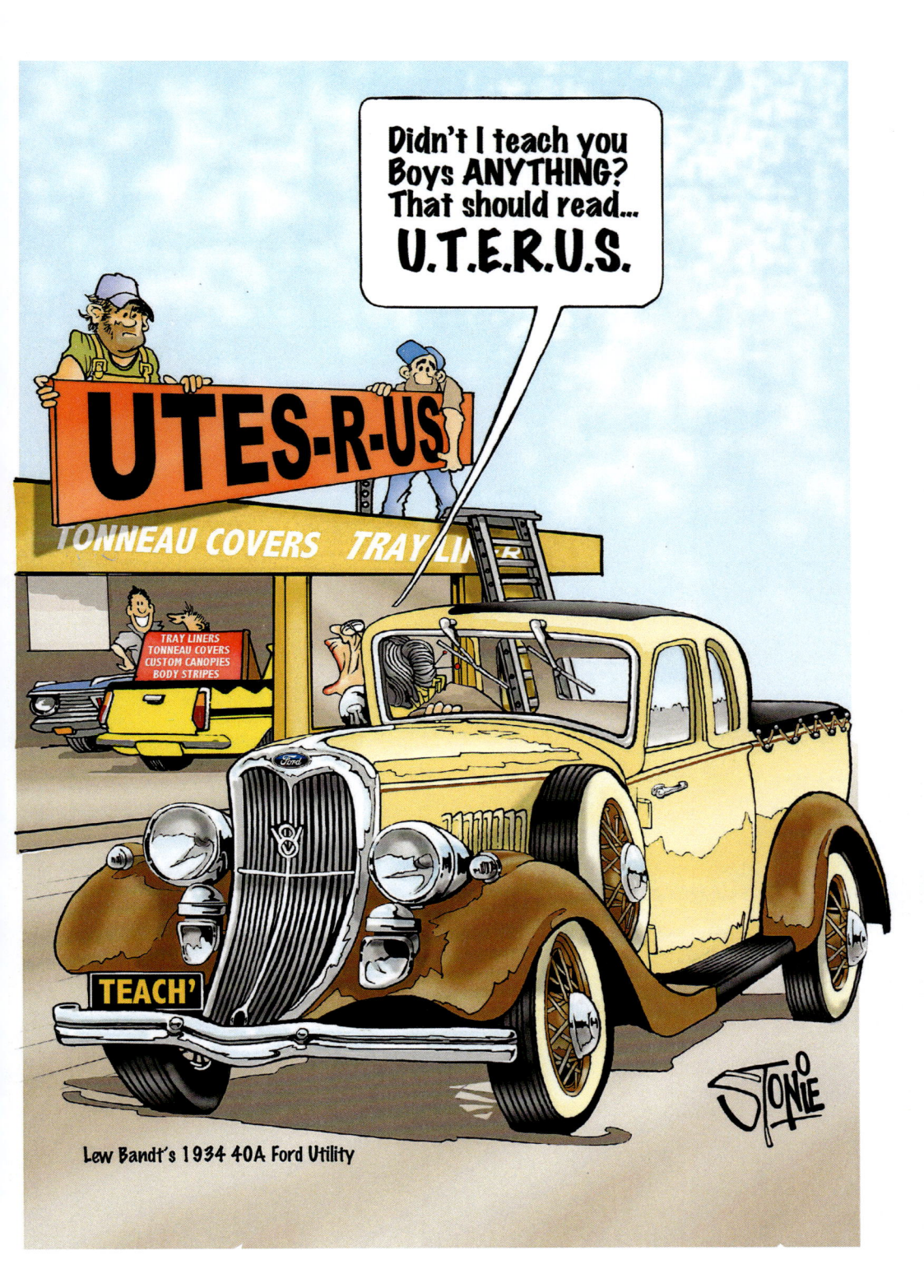

1949 Ford Pilot Sedan

After the last world war, the wounded motor industry had to gather up its skirt and get back to work. In Britain the cost of petrol and rationing made life miserable, but the stiff upper lip prevailed and some amazing cars appeared out of the bombed-out rubble.

The British Ford Pilot V8 was produced from 1947 to 1951 using a 1939 body shape that made it look out of date somewhat, except for the V8 engine.

The flathead 2.2-litre engine with three-on-the-tree column gear shift plus hydraulic brakes on the front made the V8 Brit "quite interesting", but the downside was the electrics.

Being only six volt and with the wipers vacuum-driven off the manifold, they would often stop working if you accelerated quickly. The Pilot had a certain charm, a pleasant exhaust note and it looked like a Ford Prefect deluxe on steroids with its very similar chrome grille.

You will not win a concours but it's fun to soup up the engine of a Pilot to a 1950 standard three-litre size, change the six- to a twelve-volt battery and fit electric wipers.

In Australia they were sold before they were unloaded off the boat, but when driven on the corrugated Aussie dirt roads the die-cast grille rattled loose and couldn't be repaired. The Ford dealers were so used to owners coming in with grilles in pieces, they would just swap the old grille for a new one.

Most Pilots were four-door saloons and some were made into pick-ups by Ford dealers. A token woody estate version would be a good find in a dusty barn for a canny collector! Any Pilot would make a nice unique project to restore, hotting up the mechanicals for fun.

Oh come on...
How do you get
a parking spot
with a Pilot ?
PILOT
PARKING
ONLY
HOS·TEE
1950 UK FORD PILOT V8
STONIE

1967 Volkswagen Kombi Microbus

Who would have thought any split-screen VW Kombi would have reached five-figure values in the classic car trade by the new millennium?

In the begining this commercial VW rear-engined workhorse enjoyed a love-hate following, loved by the happy campers and loathed by trade users fearful it might catch fire or flop over on its side.

The carby, coil and electrics were mounted together on top of the engine and if the spark and fuel got together, you would be invited to your own barbecue. It was around 1990 the lovable Kombi became a commercial future classic and today they are being snapped up and restored from any condition.

Be it panel van, dropsided utility or crew-cab trades van, the first split-screen Kombi is pulling crazy money. The flagship of the Kombi-class, with multiseats and observation windows in the roof, earns the title of "Microbus", the most valuable to serious collectors.

All Kombi VWs are great fun to drive on the road especially for tailgating other road users!

1967 Volkswagon Type 2 Kombi Microbus

1955 BMW Isetta Rivolta "Bubble"

Italian manufacturing company Iso was owned by individualist Renzo Rivolta who decided that making fridges and scooters wasn't enough fun and began manufacturing a microcar for the masses.

The Isetta bubble car made a sensational debut to the motoring press at Turin in 1953. Designed by Ermenegildo Preti and Pierluigi Raggi around a motorbike engine, the front panel, complete with steering wheel, opened outwards for comfortable entry for two people, and ventilation was available by sliding the fabric roof open.

This big-little bubble car could return 58mpg. Entered in the famous Mille Miglia road race, it won first, second and third in the economy class averaging 43mpg...Woo hoo!

Renzo wanted more and sold the licence and the Isetta body tooling to Germany's BMW in 1955 and then further licences to carmakers in France and Brazil. Renzo could now build his dream car, the Iso Rivolta sports muscle car with a 5.4-litre Chevy under the bonnet.

BMW beefed up the Isetta to 300cc and it became the best-selling single cylinder on the planet with 161,720 total units. Isettas under other licences evolved into vans, utes and half-ton trucks!

BMW ISETTA 250 1955   Neapolitan Mastiff

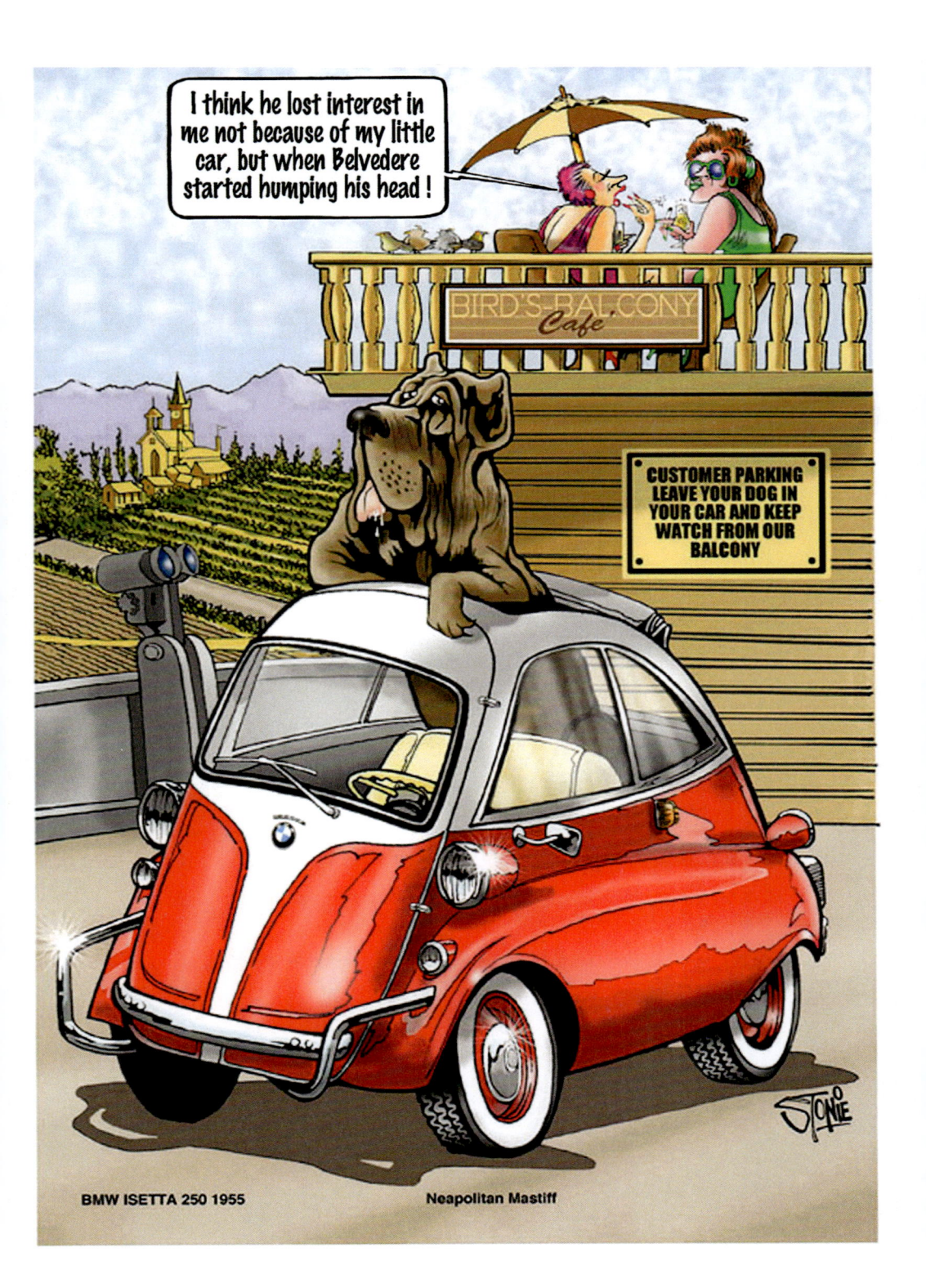

1957 Morris Isis Overdrive 6

The first Morris Isis six was made before the war (1929-35). The 1955-57 Morris Isis was no shrinking violet with a new lazy 90mph straight-six cylinder C-series engine. It shared the same body shape as the Morris Oxford, but was lengthened to fit the Isis 2.6-litre engine from the Austin A95 Westminster.

The four-speed column shift also came with a BorgWarner overdrive plus an automatic version on the Series II as an optional extra. The Isis was a very comfortable town and country long distance cruiser.

The name Isis was either from a type of rose or from the Egyptian fertility goddess Isis meaning "throne", as she wore a model of a throne on her head. These days ISIS has a more sinister meaning, and is not a good selling point.

Only 12,000 Morris Isis versions were produced, so Morris-dancing tragics may find classic prices higher than expected.

The Morris Oxford/Isis body shape lived on for many decades as the famous Indian diesel taxi, known as the Hindustan Ambassador. Isis in India means "sacred cow".

1957 MORRIS ISIS 6 CYL. OVERDRIVE

1956 Alfa Romeo Giulietta Spider

Once in our life every one of us should own an Alfa Romeo. The image of the marque makes it the ultimate romantic sports car. Not many carmakers put passion before bean counters who often say, "You can't make it like that, it's too expensive!" For Alfa passion comes first.

In 1955, Alfa Romeo was keen to expand its production capacity across the Atlantic, and the USA Alfa Romeo importer asked for a new convertible because the Yanks like to put the hood down.

Italian designer of the Giulietta Sprint Coupé, Giovanni Bertone, was asked to submit a Spider design. Always looking for the right romance in their cars, Alfa also asked Pininfarina's Franco Martinengo to pick up the pen, too.

Bertone's futuristic rounded, flowing design was very close to the yet-to-be-designed E-Type Jaguar with covered bullet headlights. Pininfarina's design was more classic fifties with blobs of chrome sculpture and traditional headlights to match the vintage Alfa grille.

Alfa went for Franco's penmanship because it reminded them of the Lancia Aurelia B24 Spider with amore and passione. The Giulietta Spider sold well and looks as classica today as when it rolled off the production line in 1956. Bravo Franco!

A famous Alfa Romeo image was of Dustin Hoffman driving a red Alfa Spider Duetto 1600 in the spicy movie *The Graduate*.

Put the top down on the 1956 Giulietta, turn up the radio and sing *See You Later Alligator* with Bill Haley and His Comets or scream along with Little Richard's *Long Tall Sally!*

1956 Vettura Alfa Romeo Giulietta 1300 Spider

The First Corvette by Chevrolet

The Midas touch of both irrepressible Harley Earl (of GM) and Lee Iaccoca (of Ford) created the automobiles people wanted. The early fifties saw Ford's two-seater Thunderbird convertible capture the imagination of the war-weary Vets for whom life was then a sports car.

Harley Earl pushed GM to allow him to build a two-seater sports to bite into the Thunderbird market share. Rather like the WWII Navy destroyer, the name Corvette was a good weapon to start with. The Harley Earl styling touch had "wow factor", the usual flare with step-up rear wings, full-blown fenders and eye-popper tail lights. Exhaust pipes were poked through the body and the recessed plate mount was glass-covered. The rounded front had the growling dog grille that said, "Get off my road!"

Harley showed the prototype to an excited public at the 1953 GM Motorama in January at the Waldorf Astoria and hysteria followed as production was rushed to stay within the model year.

The first 300 were pretty much hand-built. The body was moulded in a new concept, reinforced glass fibre, like the prototype. They said they did it to meet the deadlines rather than because of a steel shortage as rumoured at the time. The interior was classic blood red and all Corvettes came in polo-white duco.

A whistle-blower leaked the reason they were available in white only was that they had not quite got the preparation right with the fibreglass body, and white duco hid the ripples and bumps on the paint finish.

The big bits underneath were a bit of a forties' drivetrain with a straight-six engine bolted to a two-speed auto plus drum brakes for anchors. The result was a boulevard cruiser that handled like a truck.

GM executives were seriously thinking of dumping the Corvette after one year but the first new Chevy V8 arrived with a three-speed manual gearbox and the acceptance by the buying public of a plastic fantastic body... saved the Vette'.

Later, product placement in the hit TV series *Route 66* was just marketing GOLD!

1953 CHEVROLET CORVETTE

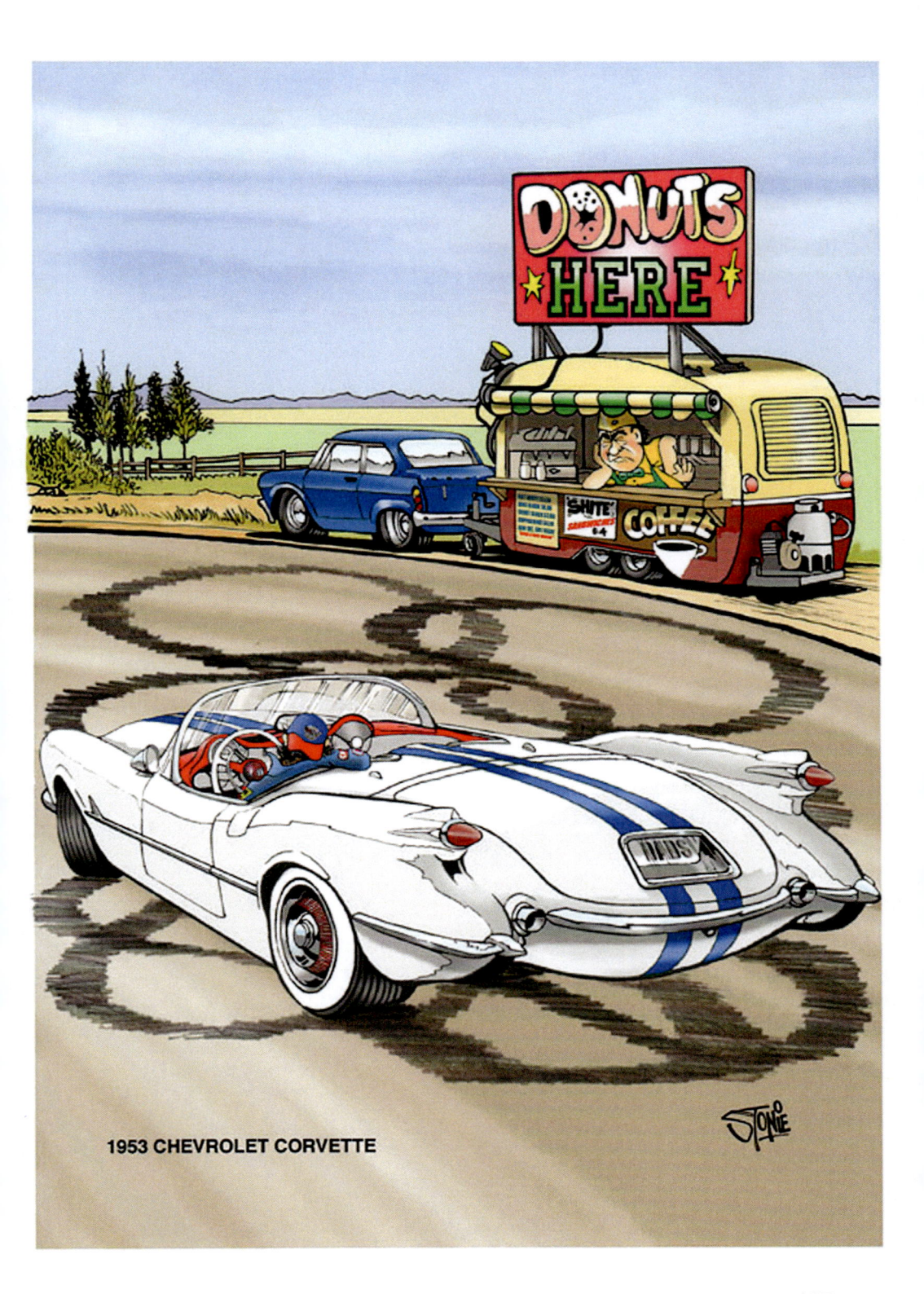

Why on God's earth would you buy your ex-mother-inlaw a bloody Jaguar ?
...worked a treat, it bit her head clean off !
MARK II
STONIE

Comrade...it's the world's best.."b-e-s-t" car awards, not WORST !
WORLDS BEST CAR
STONIE
Trabant

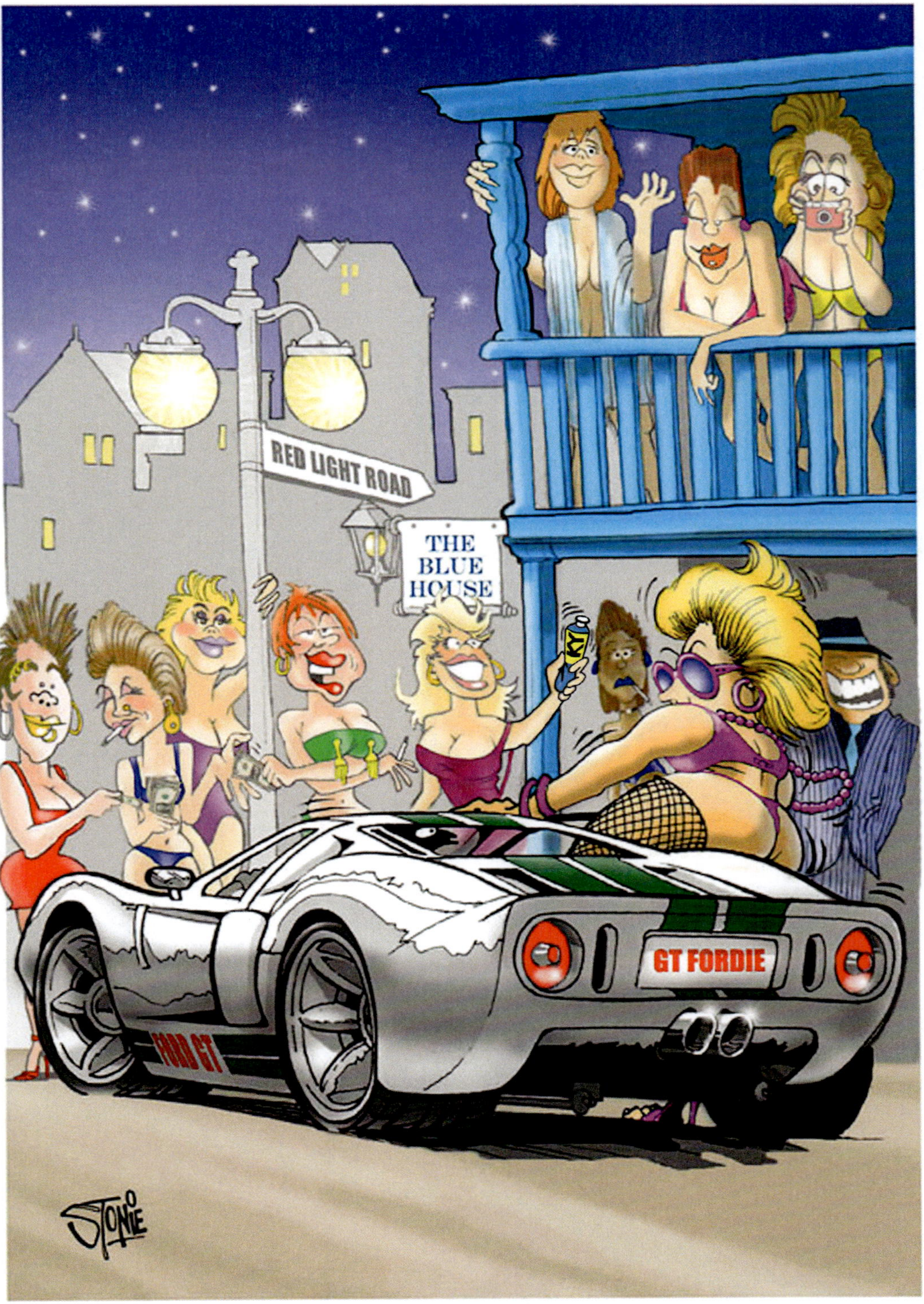
RED LIGHT ROAD
THE BLUE HOUSE
KY
GT FORDIE
FORD GT
STONIE

WATCH OUT!
LOW
FLYING
CARS

RALLY
117
...KEEP GOING
KEEP GOING !!!
STONIE

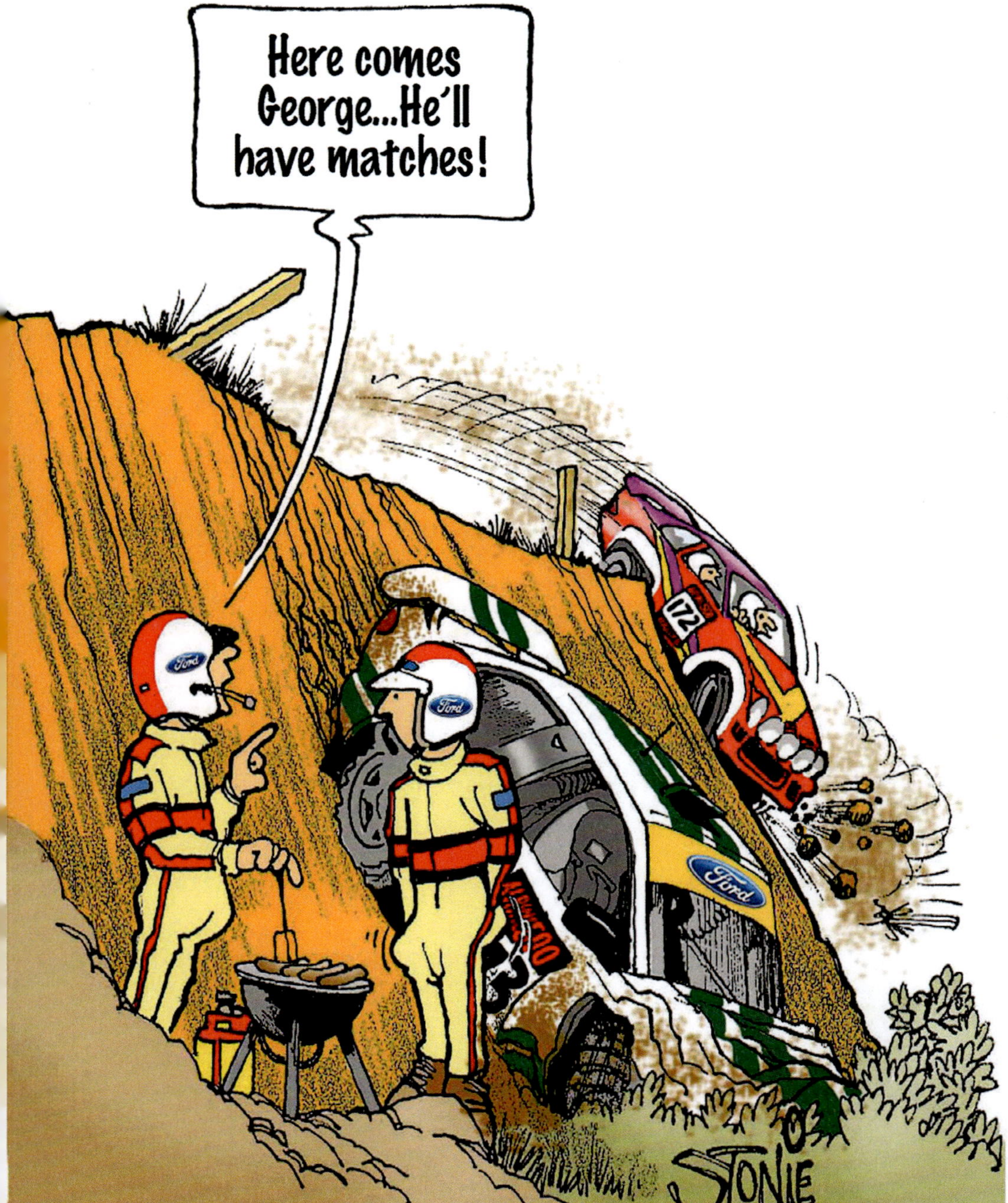
Here comes George...He'll have matches!
172
STONIE

1936 BMW 328 Roadster

Motor manufacturers around the world all have their own distinctive culture which is illustrated in the personality of the cars they produce. French, British, American, German, Swedish and Japanese car marques all have colourful histories to match.

In the mid-1930s before things got a bit hectic in Europe, an aircraft engine and motorcycle manufacturer, Bayerische Motoren Werke (BMW, meaning "Bavarian Motor Works), produced a sports roadster in true Bavarian tradition to appeal to the customer with discerning tastes. The BMW 328 Sports Roadster outmanoeuvred the opposing market without hoo-ha, with justified results to match the product.

The 328 all-alloy body on a steel chassis was propelled by an alloy straight-six two-litre engine through a four-speed gearbox. The typical thirties' style body was flanked by equally 1930s fenders with a long kidney-shaped radiator front grille. A simple badge mounted above the grille with the black roundel BMW and the centre logo was a clipping of the blue and white Bavarian national flag, but was rumoured to also signify an aeroplane propeller seeing the blue sky while spinning.

From the start, BMW cars made no bones about it, their image was motorsport and their results are testimony to their culture. Introduced at the 1936 Eifelrennen Race at the Nurburgring, the 328 won the two-litre class. 100 class wins in 1937 included the RAC Tourist Trophy, Ostereichische Alpenfahrt and la Turbie Hillclimb. They also won, in 1938, two-litre classes at Le Mans, the Alpine Rally and the Mille Miglia, and in 1939 were fifth overall at the Le Mans 24-Hour Race, also winning the two-litre class. A 328 won the 1940 Mille Miglia at an average speed of 103.6 mph.

The 328 became the first car to win both the Mille Miglia in 1940 and the Classic Historic Mille Miglia in 2004.

Frank Pratt also won the 13th Australian Grand Prix at Point Cook RAAF base in 1948 in a 328.

Many assumed for years that BMW stood for Bavarian Motorsports Works because of their motor racing successes.

1936 BMW 328 ROADSTER SIX

1961-71 Jaguar E-Type Series I & II

"It's the most beautiful car I've ever seen!" So supposedly said Enzo Ferrari, but few ask who designed the E-Type Jag. Well, it was a Malcolm Sayer, born in Norfolk, worked for Bristol Aeroplanes during the war and studied in Iraq, of all places. He met a German professor there who conveyed to him the connection of mathematics to curves and shapes.

Returning to England, Sayer joined Jaguar in 1951, preferring to be called an industrial designer rather than a "stylist"; he said he wasn't a "hairdresser"! Sayer's list starts with the C-Type, followed by the D-Type, then the E-Type. He obviously applied the maths of curves and shapes well!

Due to be launched in Geneva in March 1961, the E-Type display car was late being completed for the motor show. Jaguar executive, Bob Berry therefore had to drive the E-Type to the Parc des Eaux Vives and arrived only 20 minutes before the E-Type was due to be unveiled.

The media then complained that Jaguar didn't have a car for the press to drive and give their impressions of. William Lyons demanded a roadster be finished and sent immediately. Norman Dewis hurriedly prepared the car and drove through the night to Geneva. *AutoCar* boasted they were able to get the E-Type to do 150mph. I think this was motoring scribe imagination... it just felt like it.

The Series I E-Type flat-floor 3.8 litre seems to be the collectors' choice. Some Series One and a Half 4.2-litre E-Types had open headlights for better beam throw and the Series II had the indicators and tail lights below the bumpers for the US market.

Sadly, the E-Type remembered most in the movies was the dude wearing a crash helmet driving a white E-Type in *Vanishing Point*. He ran off the road into a river trying to race the star, Barry Newman, in a white Dodge Challenger!

You could turn on the car radio in the E-Type in 1961 and hear *Hit the Road Jack* by Ray Charles or sing along with Ricky Nelson to *Travelin' Man*.

1970 Jaguar E-Type Series II

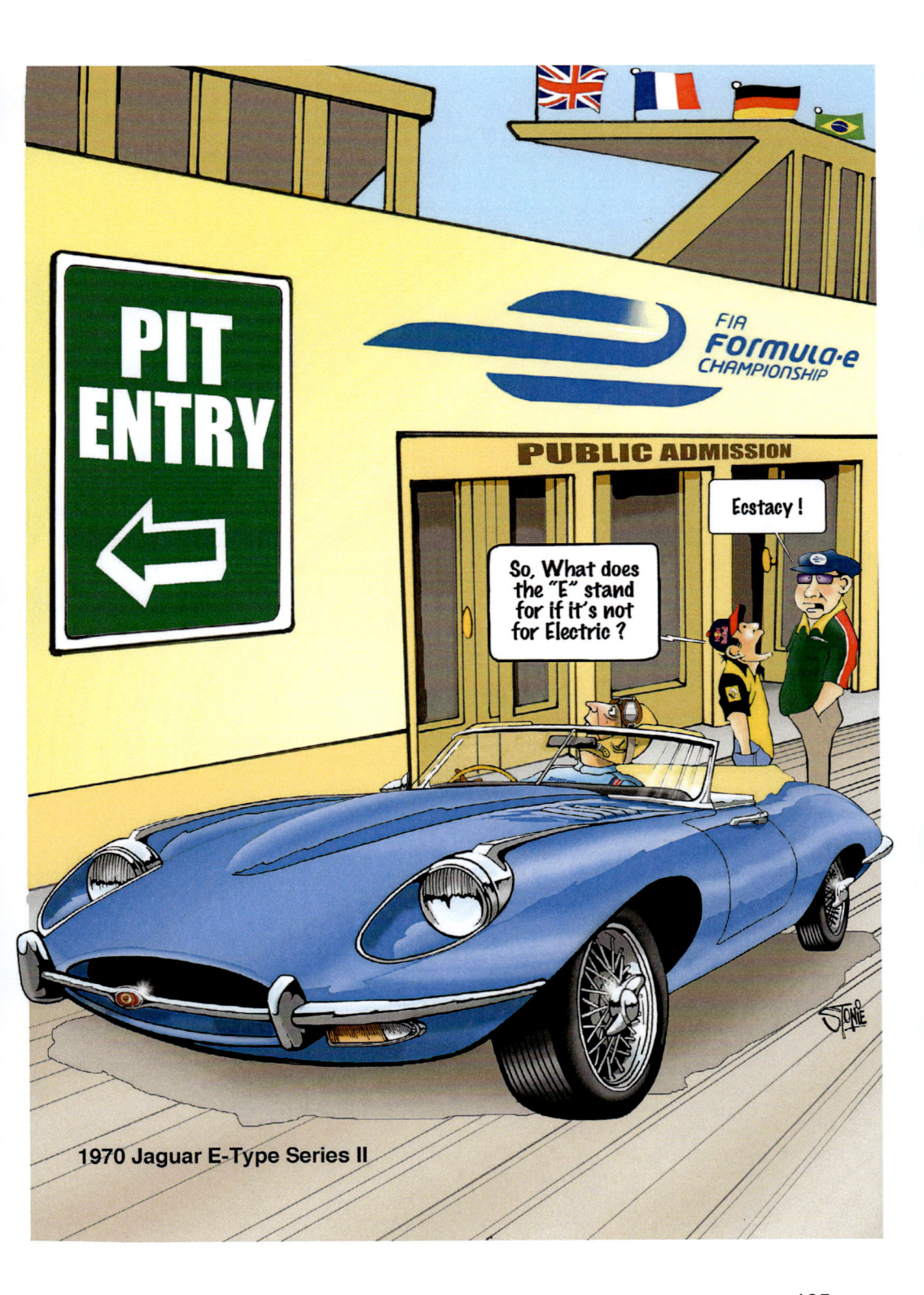

1963-77 Alpine Renault A110 Coupé

A dedicated production "speciale" rally car way before the Lancia Stratos, the Alpine A110 Renault (pronounced "Alpeen") ticks all the competition boxes and has the victories to prove it. Son of a Renault dealer, Jean Rédélé had the passion and conviction to build such a serious rally special plus produce a model range of lookalike road cars, similar to what Ford did with the GT40 dedicated racing and road cars.

Christened the Berlinette, the Alpine's aggressive coupé final design was by Giovanni Michelotti (who also designed the Triumph TR4 and five sports cars). The story goes Rédélé sketched out the basic shape on a napkin over dinner and a bottle of wine. No pretty wings or fancy bits on the Alpine, just built-in front long-range rally lights and safety purpose external competition isolation switches on the left back fender to shut down the engine. There was, however, a first prototype A108 with a Renault R8 Gordini motor which was produced in Brazil by Willys.

Later, when the road cars were produced, the only difference really was that they didn't have the competition front seats. Only enthusiasts needed apply for the competition special, as the growling engine was not for the faint-hearted.

Instantly, the Alpine started winning rallies in France, and in the seventies, reached international status in the Championship for Manufacturers, including a great 1-2-3 in the 1971 Monte Carlo Rally under the guidance of Swedish rally ace Ove Andersson.

"Alpeen" was bought out by Renault and became the first winner of the World Rally Championship in 1973.

In 1994 a Renault Alpine won the classic Millers Oil RAC Rally Britannia.

A new modern-day A110 Alpine was released onto the market in 2018: a 1.8-litre turbo engine with a seven-speed Getrag gearbox and, of course, with the signature integrated driving lights in the nose. You would expect the modern Alpine to do well on the modern tarmac rally circuits.

1969 ALPINE RENAULT A-110

He had to come in...He dropped biscuit crumbs in his crotch !
CAR VAC
24 HEURES
117
STONIE

NEW HOUSE
THE WIFE'S
117
STONIE

"AAH! WHAT IS INSTRUCTION FOR BIG HOLE?"
DATSUN
DATSUN
TOTAL OIL
7
CIBIE
CIBIE
7
STONIE

1956 BMW 507 V8 Roadster

By the end of the 1940s BMW had been allowed to restart making motorcycles and small cars after the British Bristol Car Company was given licence to use pre-war BMW body styles and engines. After a gentle toe in the water with 501 and 502 sedans and the smooth straight-six and V8 engines, BMW targeted the US market to put some Deutschmarks back in the piggy bank.

Watching the Mercedes-Benz 300SL sales in the US and, pushed by their US car importer, Max Hoffman, BMW enlisted the drawing board skills of German-American, Count Albrecht von Goertz, to come up with a sports car design. The result was the 507 Sports Roadster V8 and by the end of 1956, 34 507s were produced.

This very traditional classic design alloy body had a smooth alloy V8 under the bonnet. Notably, the 507 had multiple BMW badges on it, one on each of the five wheel-spinners, on each of the two vents on the front fenders, on the bonnet and in the centre of the steering wheel.

Launched at the Waldorf Astoria in New York, in 1955, production began in 1956. While some notable Americans bought the 507 at $US5,000, sales were not great so that took BMW to the edge of bankruptcy.

Elvis Presley bought his white 507 in Germany while serving in the US Army, but the fräulein fans put lipstick marks all over it, so he painted it red to match the lipstick. When he returned to the US he bought another 507 and gave the red one to Ursula Andress, his co-star on the set of the movie *Fun in Acapulco*. Ursula's husband, John Derek, already had a 507 and sold his to Fred Astaire.

Formula One boss, Bernie Ecclestone sold his 507 in 2007 at auction for £904,000. Only 202 BMW 507 cars are known to exist today.

Elvis Presley had several big hits in 1956 including *Blue Suede Shoes, Heartbreak Hotel, Hound Dog* and *Don't be Cruel*. The film *Love Me Tender* was released at that time.

1956 BMW 507 V8 ROADSTER

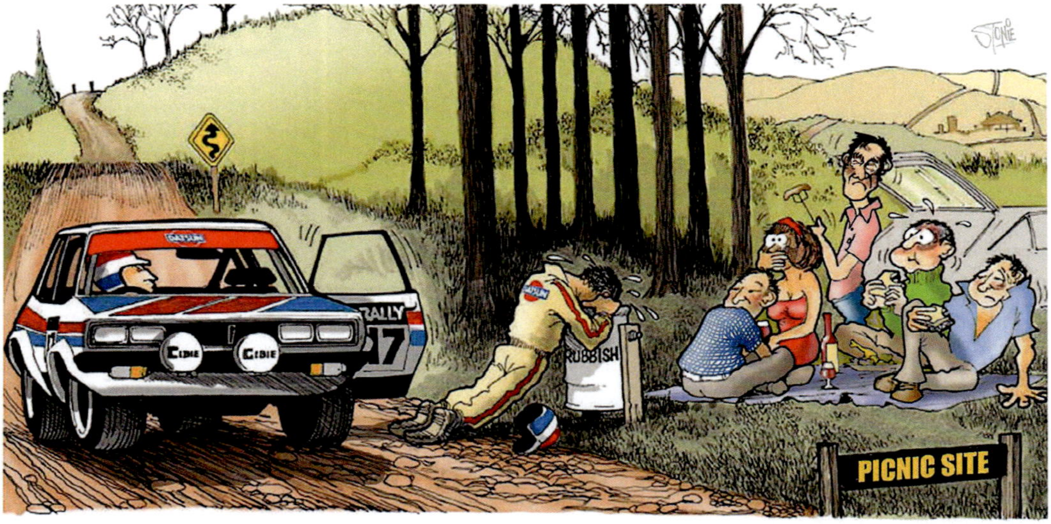

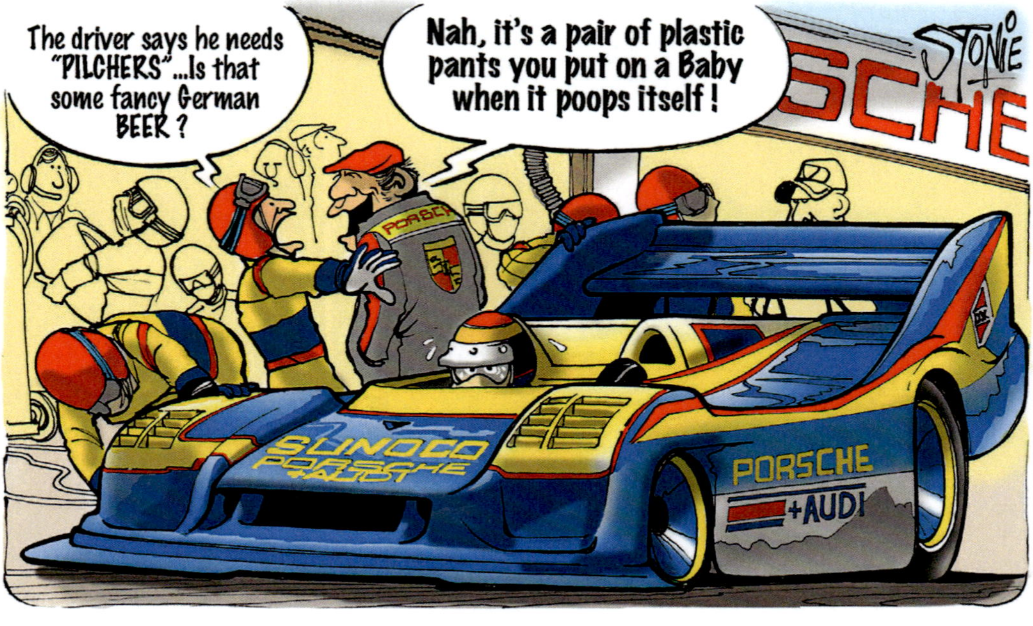

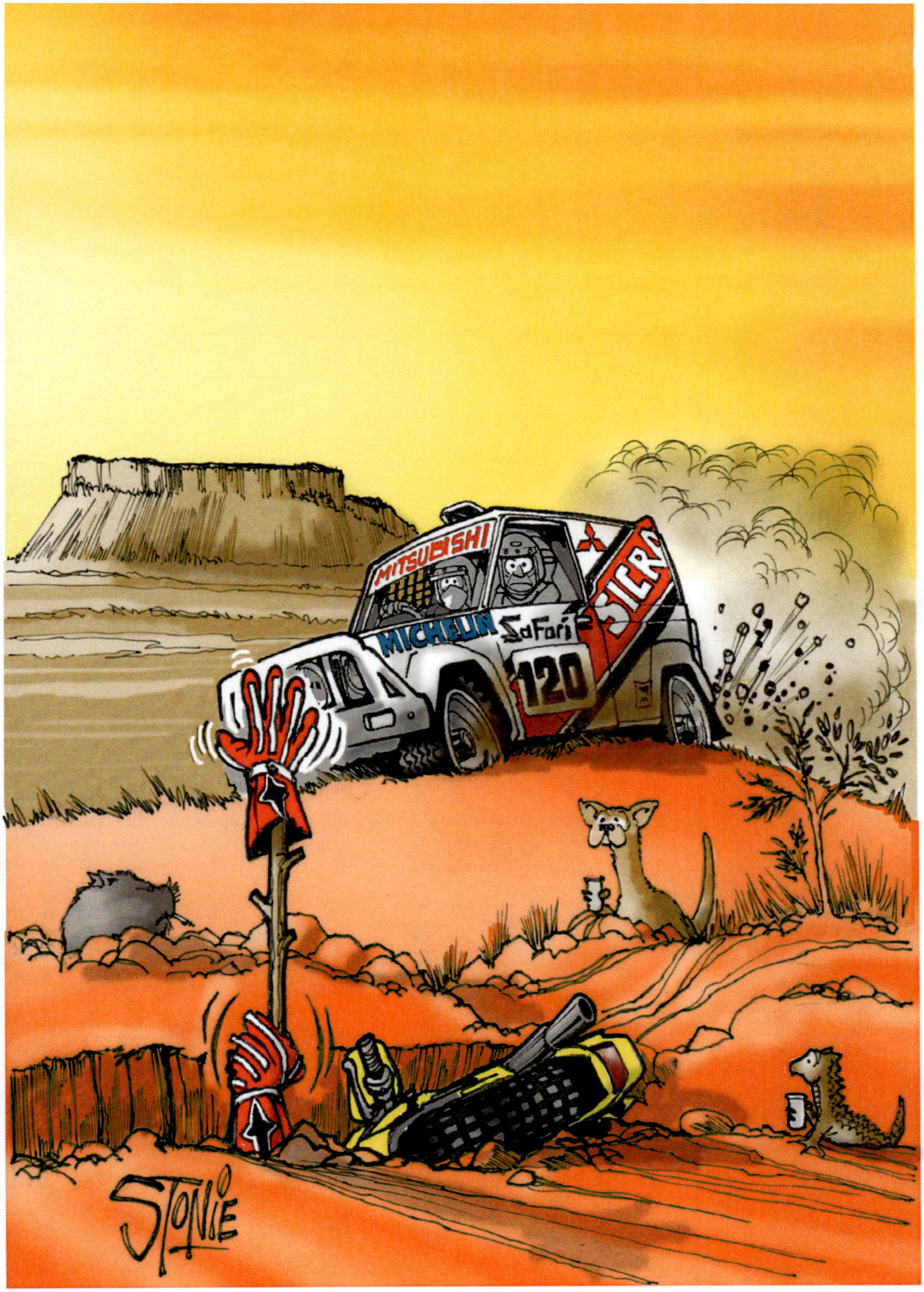
MITSUBISHI
MICHELIN
SaFari
120
STONIE

Jaguar XK120 Roadster

Many will say the real beginning of the Jaguar legend was with the William Lyons XK engine and the XK120. Deemed the fastest production car of the day, a prototype was tested in 1949 on a closed motorway used in the RAC of Belgium Rally where it was clocked at 132.6mph. Race and rally wins proved the XK120 was the car to choose for anything to do with speed.

One fascinating story is that, while living in Melbourne Australia, Nevil Shute, author of the book *On the Beach,* did some race driving research for the character who kills himself in a car race at the end, played by Fred Astaire in the Stanley Kramer movie.

Some speculation is rife that Shute made a cameo appearance in the movie's race scene. Australian race car driver, Murray Carter was racing an XK120 (with a Corvette six-cylinder in it, tut, tut!) at Fishermens Bend circuit in Melbourne Australia when he chatted to this fellow XK120 driver in the pits who was asking all sorts of questions about race driving. It appears he was researching material for a book and his name was Nevil Shute. Later, other race drivers in Melbourne confirmed Shute was well known in Melbourne in those days.

You can easily tell the difference between the XK120 and XK140. The 13-bar grille on the XK120 was far too expensive to produce on the XK140, so a cast iron seven-bar grille was the replacement.

1952 JAGUAR XK120 ROADSTER

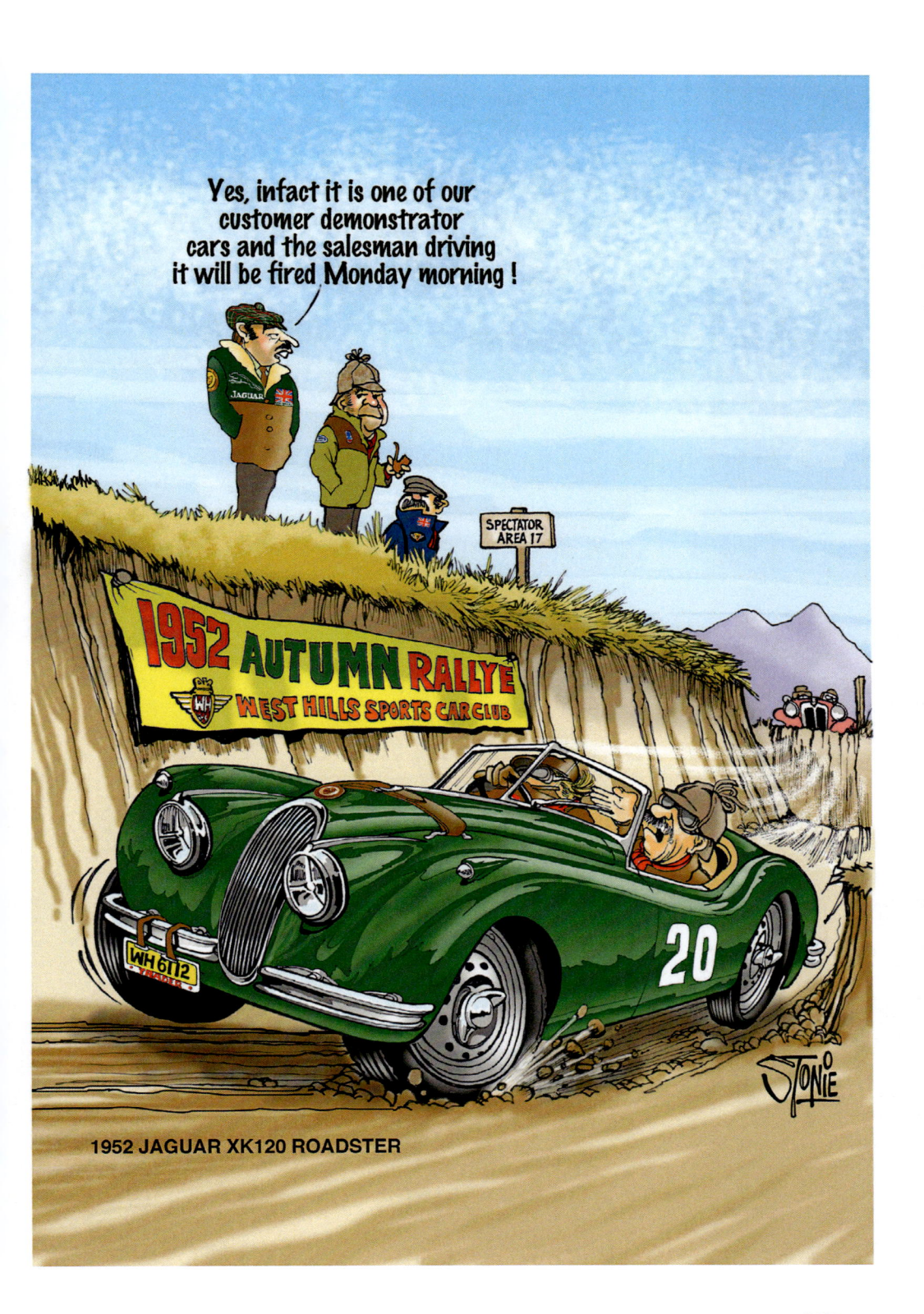

TRY NOT
TO RUN
OVER THE
MINIS

You wanna' eat the Mini Woody for dinner ?
I couldn't, I had a Morgan for lunch!
WOODY
STONIE

STONIE
Started building a P40 Kittyhawk but ran out of shed-room !
P40

Well... Your bum will look smaller in the **NEW MINI !**
STONIE
50 YEARS OF MINI
NEW M
1959

Come on Guys... Where's my real Hornet ?
WOLSELEY
STONIE

I said...Drive it like you own it ! NOT...drive it like you stole it !
INSTRUCTOR
Castrol
JIM RUSSELL
SCHOOL OF DRIVING TECHNIQUE
STONIE

1966 Morris Cooper S Type

Other car manufacturers can only dream of the product placement the Mini received in the Michael Caine movie, *The Italian Job*. Also, in the first scenes of the motor racing movie *Winning*, Paul Newman and Joanne Woodward were seen belting around in a Mini Cooper S.

Peter Sellers had a specially built Mini Cooper with wicker chair side panels worth £2,600. George Harrison, Mick Jagger and Twiggy all had Mini Coopers and Rowan Atkinson's character Mr Bean sort of promoted the Mini with his lemon Morris Mini 850 with a black bonnet!

The real Mini story is the development of the Mini Cooper. Race car builder and Formula One world championship constructor John Cooper and his father, used BMC engines in their Formula Junior cars. Even before the new Mini was released, Cooper, a friend of the creator Alec Issigonis, wanted to get his hands on the new buzz bomb.

Specifically aiming at class wins in Touring Car GT racing, Cooper changed the 850cc block, bore & stroke to 997cc. The gearbox ratios were also changed along with additions like twin SU carbies, remote gear shift, extractor exhaust and front-disc brakes. Issigonis was thrilled and collaborated with Cooper for another class-winning engine size later, the 1071cc model.

They then plotted for a 1300cc weapon called the Cooper S Type with nitrided crank and bigger power-assisted front discs. The new engine was a 1275cc as the premium class competitor, along with a 970cc screamer which only lasted for a short time. The Coopers also had added comfort of carpets and a fan-assisted heater but alas no tachometer. A special lightweight magnesium wheel was even made for the racing Minis called a Minilite.

Issigonis was a good friend of Enzo Ferrari and he "gave" a Mini Cooper to the famous marque originator who thrashed around the Modena hills for medicinal purposes only. Cooper was a groundbreaker in combining a motor sport name with a car model. Lotus Cortina, Fiat Abarth and Shelby Mustang followed and the list goes on.

John Cooper was paid a royalty believed to be £2 a car. I wonder if BMW, who now build modern Mini Coopers, still pay the family two quid a car!-

1966 Morris "MINI" Cooper S

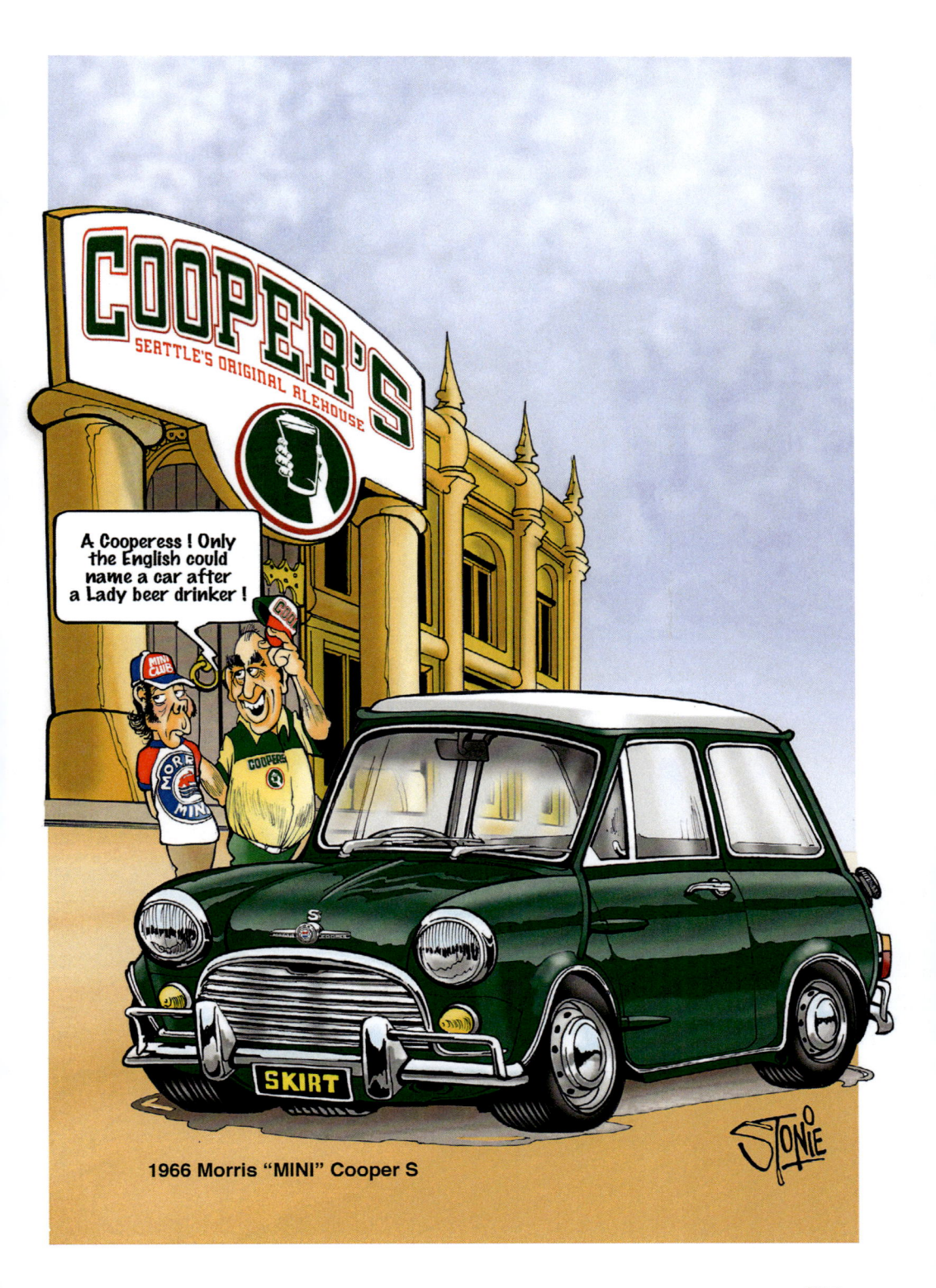

I can't believe you and I ever fitted in one of these things 45 years ago
You didn't have a spare tyre then Darl'
STONIE

STONIE
FOLLOW ME!
RAF BASE

Car 19 has lost second place and really dragging his feet !
19
STONIE

WRONG GRILLE!
MINI OWNERS ODD BALL-DAY
minimix
CON'S CRETE
"NO JOB TOO SMAll"
CONMIX
STONIE

INDEX

1936 Aston Martin Le Mans 2 litre	Page 14
1938 MG Keller SA Type 2.3 litre Straight 6	Page 18
1948 Ford Tudor Coupe V8 'Single Spinner'	Page 20
1938-49 Ford Prefect	Page 26
1967 Triumph TR5 PI – TR250	Page 28
1954 Buick Wildcat II Concept Car	Page 30
1960-63 Chevrolet Corvair	Page 32
1957 Ford Mercury Turnpike V8	Page 34
1957 Jaguar XK 140	Page 38
1948 Morris Minor MM Series Lowlight	Page 40
1967-68 Pontiac Firebird	Page 42
1958 Nash Rambler Metropolitan	Page 44
1951 Studebaker Commander "Bullet Nose"	Page 46
1968 Austin Healey MKIII 3000	Page 50
1953 Bristol 404	Page 52
1955 Rolls-Royce Dawn	Page 54
1938 Alfa Romeo 8C Superleggera	Page 56
1960 Renault Floride Convertible	Page 58
1970 Pontiac GTO "The Judge"	Page 60
1966-71 GT40 Ford	Page 66
1947-52 Austin of England A40 Devon-Dorset	Page 68
1952 Hudson Hornet Hollywood Coupe	Page 70
1953-59 The Cadillac "Big Years"	Page 72
1957 Cadillac Eldorado Biarritz Convertible	Page 74
1936 Ford V8 Coupe	Page 76
1965 Oldsmobile Toronado FWD	Page 78
1975 Porsche 930 Turbo	Page 80
1989 Nissan Figaro	Page 82
1957 Chevrolet Belair	Page 84
1934 Voisin C15 Saloit Roadster	Page 86
Father of the Mustang – Lee Iacocca	Page 88
1953 General Motors-Holden FJ	Page 90
1955 Volkswagen Karmann Ghia	Page 92
1960 Goggomobile DART	Page 94
1966 Bedford TJ Series	Page 96
1959 Holden FC Special	Page 98

1935 Ford V8 Deluxe Roadster	Page 100
1965 Pontiac Bonneville Convertible	Page 102
1969 Holden Monaro GTS 350 Coupé	Page 104
1955 Mercedes-Benz 300 SL Coupé	Page 106
1958 Austin Healey MKI Sprite	Page 108
1933 Duesenberg SJ Speedster	Page 112
1966-72 Lamborghini Miura	Page 114
Corvettes, Stingrays and TV's Route 66	Page 116
1965 Aston Martin DB5	Page 118
1968 Fiat 500D	Page 120
1964 Volvo P1800S	Page 122
1973 Rover P5B Coupé V8	Page 124
1913 Morgan Vee-Twin 3-Wheeler	Page 126
The Bentley and the "Angel-Box"	Page 128
1960 Chrysler New Yorker and the Drive	Page 130
1929 Austin Seven "Chummy"	Page 134
1929 Roosevelt Marmon	Page 136
1962-64 Ferrari GTO 250	Page 138
1960 Daimler SP250 V8	Page 140
Datsun 240Z & Toyota 2000 GT	Page 142
1948-58 Land Rover Series I	Page 144
1954 Facel Vega Series II	Page 146
1928 Chevrolet National 4	Page 150
1949-61 Morris Commercial J-Type Van	Page 152
1959 Firebird III "Blister" Prototype	Page 154
The Anderson Detroit Electric Car	Page 156
1948 Chevrolet Fleetmaster Woodie Wagon	Page 158
1969-72 Holden Torana GTR & XU-1	Page 160
1938 DKW 700cc Twin Utility	Page 162
1941 Willys/Ford "Jeep"	Page 164
1929 Hudson Super Six	Page 166
1960 MGA Twin Cam & 1966 MGB	Page 168
1928 Willys Falcon Knight Roadster	Page 170
1966 Aston Martin DB6 II Volante	Page 172
1934 Ford Utility V8 "Kangaroo Chaser"	Page 174
1949 Ford Pilot Sedan	Page 176
1967 Volkswagen Kombi Microbus	Page 178
1955 BMW Isetta Rivolta "Bubble"	Page 180
1957 Morris Isis Overdrive 6	Page 182
1956 Alfa Romeo Giulietta Spider	Page 184
The First Corvette by Chevrolet	Page 186
1936 BMW 328 Roadster	Page 192
1961-71 Jaguar E-Type Series I & II	Page 194
1963-77 Alpine Renault A110 Coupé	Page 196
1956 BMW 507 V8 Roadster	Page 200
Jaguar XK120 Roadster	Page 204
1966 Morris Cooper S Type	Page 208